MW00443322

Life from Both Sides Now

Living and Loving a Transgender Life Together

Jan and Diane DeLap

Halo
PUBLISHING
INTERNATIONAL

ISBN: 978-1-63765-162-9
LCCN: 2021925726

Halo Publishing International, LLC
www.halopublishing.com

Printed and bound in the United States of America

To Jan—Forever, my love.

Our 50th-anniversary celebration.

For the best and brightest
grandchildren anyone could have.

Contents

Introduction

"Both Sides Now" was a pop song written and made popular in the late 1960s by Joni Mitchell. At several points in the song, she mentions looking at things from "both sides." She looks at clouds, love, and life from "both sides," remembers "illusions" from each, and concludes that she doesn't really know any of them.

Jan and I were both born during the World War II era, and in the '60s we married and started a family. We were also dealing with looking at life from both male and female genders. We really, at that time, did not know how our lives would turn out. I was transgender—experiencing both genders—although the term *transgender*[1] did not exist in popular vernacular or understanding yet. Jan and I struggled to understand my feelings and how to integrate them into our lives while we worked, lived, and raised our family.

Many people through the years told us that we should write our story down. If this ever will become a book or be of interest to anyone else, I don't know. However, our history has some unique elements that perhaps will be lessons for others.

---

[1] For definitions of gender terms used in this book, refer to the "GLAAD Media Reference Guide—Transgender," https://www.glaad.org/reference/transgender.

One of the things I'd like to communicate to others experiencing gender conflict is that you can survive. It doesn't matter if you are ten or fifty years old; you can survive and be happy with who you are.

Jan and I talked about starting this book several times. Jan didn't want to write it, but as a lifelong editor and proof-reader, she was willing to edit it. In the end, we each wrote some sections that will be incorporated into this book. Unfortunately, Jan's struggle with inflammatory breast cancer ended at about 1:15 p.m. on July 23, 2019. I was at her side when she took her last breath.

There are really two elements of our lives that I hope I can emphasize in this book. The first is our personal history, and the second is how parts of that history were affected by my being transsexual. The second caused a break from some family members and subsequent isolation from others in the family. I hope that the personal history portions will provide our family with a background to their lives that will help them understand a bit more of their ancestry.

Fifty-four years seven months and twenty-five days. That's the length of time that Jan and I were married. She loved to say that we were "Velcroed at the hips together." We loved being together. Oh, we had our ups and downs. In fifty-four plus years, there were a lot of downs, but we struggled through them. Our love for each other, our faith in God's love for both of us, and our good senses of humor helped us survive.

Diane DeLap, 2021

My Beginnings

My earliest memories are of a happy family in which I was loved and cared for by a devoted father and mother. My birth name was William. Later in life, I found out that I was adopted twice, my first adoptive name being Frederick or Freddy. I remember events both in my first adoptive family and outside playing with neighbor children that were pleasant and happy. Those are good memories. Unfortunately, I learned early in life that "all good things can come to an end." I can remember at a very young age riding in a car with my father (I can even remember the road we were on). He told me that my mother had died. She was in heaven, he told me. I can remember looking out of the car window, up to the sky, and saying, "I don't see her. Where is she, Daddy?"

We were on our way to a relative's house where I would live for a time. The time following is a blur in my memory. I was to find out later that I was just over four years old when my mother died, and until I was placed with my second adoptive parents six months later, I was in more than five temporary homes. I remember this as being a most traumatic time. In some homes, there were other children, and, being the newest and youngest, I became a target for blame. If any of the other children did something wrong, I got blamed for it. I am sure that I was a problem also because I had lost my whole family at a very young age and had to learn quickly to rely on myself only.

The whole situation probably made me somewhat uncommunicative, unruly, and generally difficult to handle. During a pre-adoption interview for my second adoptive parents, my new mother told the social worker that "the child was very much spoiled when he came into the home, and it took intelligent handling to correct some of his faults." Her statement was very meaningful, as I was to find out. Her "intelligent handling" took the form of physical and verbal abuse that lasted until I left home fourteen years later to enter the Navy. When I was adopted a second time, I was named Edward and nicknamed Teddy or Ted. I often had to explain that Ted is a nickname for Edward in the New England area, giving the example of Senator Edward Kennedy, whose nickname was well known to be Ted.

A New Home

My second adoptive parents were both about forty-five when I arrived, older than most parents of a four-year-old. My new mother was British, having been born early in the first decade of the 1900s in India, the daughter of a British contractor there. She, her brother, and her mother returned to England, and she received her education in the best private schools. They left England for the United States after WWI, and they moved to California and into a small, quiet community near Los Angeles called Beverly Hills. The movie industry was getting its start, and my new mother got some small roles in silent movies. She had been a well-known dancer and teacher in England, and her experience with Eastern dances gained as a young child in India gave her a useful talent for some of the early sheikh-type movies. Her scrapbook shows that she became friends with some of the famous screen stars of her time. She corresponded with them for many years.

For some reason, she and her mother decided to move to Boston, where she worked for a large business machine company. Before working for that company, she worked for a short time in a bank. When the bank merged with a larger bank in Boston, she met the young bank clerk whom she would marry. After serving as a bicycle messenger boy in Boston in his teens, my new father became a bank clerk when he was twenty years old. His father died when he was a young boy, and his mother remarried; they lived on the North Shore of Boston. Following my new parents' marriage in 1936, they bought a home in Waltham and moved there in 1939.

My mother was a volunteer with the Red Cross, and, one day in 1946, my first adoptive father came to the office and told the story that his wife had died and he was looking for a family to adopt their child. She spoke to her husband that night, and they decided that they would take me for a trial period.

When I arrived, they had been married about ten years, with no children. My mother, in the British tradition of child-rearing, was strict. My father was of the opinion that parental responsibilities should be strictly divided. It was his responsibility to work and earn money to provide for the family and take care of the legal and financial affairs. My mother's responsibility was to take care of the house, keep it clean, provide meals with what money he would give her, and take care of me.

The day I arrived at the house, my new parents showed me my room and through the rest of the small, two-bedroom bungalow in Waltham. Shortly after I arrived, I had to go to the bathroom, and when I exited the bathroom, their English bulldog, "Monty" (named for British Field Marshal Montgomery), was standing at the door, waiting for me. The sight of this ferocious-looking bulldog scared the living daylights out of me, and I cried for help. Despite this startling introduction, Monty and I became fast friends, and I learned that he was a very gentle animal, despite his terrifying looks.

The early time I spent with my new parents was relatively calm. I was enrolled in a parochial school in Waltham, and I guess I did okay. I do remember, sometime after arriving there, going to the courthouse for the final adoption hearing. I remember a very imposing-looking judge leaning out over his large, high desk to look at me and ask me, "Do you want to live with these people?"

What was I to say? I had nowhere else to live, so, of course, I said, "Yes."

Sometime after the adoption was final, things started to get worse. Apparently, my mother decided that she would take charge, and, given that I was "spoiled" and needed "intelligent handling," she would make me do what she wanted. There were several possible reasons for what resulted. The first could be my independent attitude, resulting from several months of temporary homes. Second, her British upbringing, which traditionally meant a physical approach to child-rearing, and, finally, her age. At forty-five plus years of age, it is difficult to be patient with a rebellious five-year-old. Some friends have speculated that the onset of menopause had caused emotional changes in my mother.

My father had physical problems during this time as well. He had excruciating pain in his back from arthritis that settled in his spine and gradually calcified it. During this process, which took several years, he was in intense pain, which caused him to be very demanding of my mother. All of this caused my mother to take out the frustrations of her life on me. I cannot excuse what she did, but I did come to understand. However, understanding now as an adult doesn't change that I was a frightened, withdrawn six-year-old. I didn't know what else was going on; I just knew that my life was miserable.

My mother became physically abusive to me almost continually. I was not allowed out of the house except for school and had to come home right from school, or I would be in trouble. One time in first grade, I decided to walk home from school with some friends. When I arrived home late, my mother grabbed the most convenient thing to use to beat me. It happened to be a small baseball bat of mine (an Alvin Dark model). She proceeded to come after me with it. I dove under my bed and stayed there until she settled down. I can still remember the feeling of being under that bed and watching the bat being swept back and forth under the bed in an attempt to reach me.

Normally, things were not that bad, probably because she was concerned that the neighbors or my father would see the marks on me. Usually, she just hit me with her hand, a towel, or a strap. Her favorite method of striking me, however—and probably the thing that hurt the most—was with words. She had a biting tongue and usually just stood there and screamed and yelled at me. It was years before I understood what a "guttersnipe" was, but that was one of her favorite descriptions for me. One time I asked her what it meant; she told me that it was a homeless urchin that lived on the streets of London. Later I read Dickens and realized that she looked at me as if I were one of the unfortunate orphans in his novels.

She was fond of reminding me that she and my father were very generous in taking me in since no one wanted me. Often, she would threaten to get rid of me if I didn't obey. One time I remember her driving me to a local police station and sitting outside in the car while she told me that if I didn't promise to change my misbehaving ways, she would put me in jail.

One of the most difficult aspects of the situation was the isolation. I had very few friends. I was not allowed out of the house much, except for school, and when I did try to make friends, it was difficult to talk to them. There was no one I could talk to about my situation, and if I did, no one could do anything. I had no other place to live, so the best thing I could do was to keep my mouth shut and not complain. I tried once to tell my father about my mother's abuse, but when he talked to her about it, she denied it, saying I was exaggerating normal punishment. He accepted her version because it was her job to take care of me, and he left it alone. She responded to me by punishing me severely, so I decided that silence was the best option.

Now we get to one of the most difficult aspects of the story. All of the previous may sound pretty terrible, but there was more. One of my mother's favorite means of dealing with me was to lock me in my bedroom closet when she couldn't take anymore. Often, after a beating, she would lock me in the closet. She told me that I could not come out until I stopped crying, promised to change my ways, or admitted that whatever I had done was wrong. I was not even permitted to come out to go to the bathroom. I remember several times urinating on myself and defecating in my pants. The result made her even angrier because she had to clean my clothes, so I was put back in the closet after another beating and getting cleaned up.

One of the issues that also caused me frustration was my gender identity. At that age, I had no idea what the problem was. I just knew that I wished I were a girl. I had had the feeling that I was really a girl almost as far back as I could remember. I felt that if I were, I could please my mother. I often dreamed that something would happen that would make me a girl. I remember seeing science fiction movies and TV programs in which people could change forms and wishing that I could also change myself into a girl. Also, I felt more comfortable with girls. I often played with them in the neighborhood. I attempted to play sports, but I was never very good at any physical endeavors. I always thought that girls were better than boys and I preferred their company. For as far back as I can remember, I wished to be a girl rather than a boy. Whether it was true or not, I always felt that girls received better treatment than boys.

My isolation grew because I knew that I was different from others. I didn't feel comfortable with boys, although I tried to play sports and other games. Usually, however, I was the last one chosen for games because I was not good at them. I was also uneasy around girls because they expected me to act like the other boys, and I couldn't live up to those expectations.

I did have some experience with younger girls who lived next door when I was about ten years old. In their family, there were three girls, ranging from about eight down to five years old. We enjoyed playing together several times a week for one summer. All of our games were very innocent and typical children's games. Our play ended when the girls' parents told my parents that they felt that it was not normal for me to be playing with their girls and that I was not to play with them anymore. This experience taught me that I could not reach out to the female world without others seeing my attempt as improper and unnatural. This episode caused my further isolation.

When I was about ten years old, newspapers and televisions reported the story of Christine Jorgensen. She had traveled to Denmark and undergone hormone therapy and a series of operations that the *New York Daily News* described in a sensational article as a "sex change." This story was the first inkling I had of where I fit. The ridicule of my parents and the media made me realize that this was not anything I could do because it was not something that was acceptable. I was born a boy, and I was stuck with that. As I grew, I tried to cope with my feelings. I thought that if I could find a girl to date and eventually marry, these feelings would disappear.

After the third grade, my parents transferred me to a grade school in Belmont, Massachusetts. It was there that I had a memorable experience in cross-dressing. I was in the choir and was one of the better singers, with a boy's soprano voice. The nuns who taught at the school were having a pageant. I was designated to sing a central part, and they told me that I needed to dress in one of the nuns' habits for the performance. I objected that those were women's clothes. They assured me that the men also wore similar habits. I did my part, secretly enjoying the experience.

The physical abuse by my mother continued until I was about twelve years old. I learned to minimize the effects by not crying and standing still while she beat me. This approach sometimes angered her because she said that she wasn't "getting through" to me. But if I cried and pleaded for her forgiveness, it was worse because she said I was weak and she needed to "make a man" out of me. The event that marked the end of the physical abuse was my first experience with retaliation. I was getting older and stronger, and my retaliation was strong enough to make her think twice about hitting me again.

This incident started like any of hundreds of previous experiences. When my mother was angry with me about some real or perceived misdeed of mine, she would come into my room, tell me to stand up, and begin to hit me about the head and upper body. This time, as she struck me repeatedly, the force of her attack drove me back into the corner of my room. As she continued to hit me, there in the corner, I became afraid for my life. I swung at her in self-defense, with my head down, and struck her with full force on the breast.

Her reaction was immediate. She cried out in pain, stopped hitting me, and ran out of the room in tears. I immediately was filled with remorse and ran after her, apologizing for hitting her. My father came home from work later, and when she told him that I had struck her, he became angry and punished me. This incident at least established that I could fight back, and she never struck me in the same way again.

Of course, that didn't mean that her verbal abuse ended. Until the day I left the house to enter the Navy, she continued to stand at my bedroom door and criticize me for my many faults. I learned to turn her off and ignore her barrage of words. I will never forget that her favorite phrase, "I'm not going to say anything else about the matter," meant exactly the opposite. It meant that she was pausing to catch her breath and that she would be back in less than five minutes to take up the discourse again.

An incident that illustrates the depth of the frustration I experienced listening to her tirades occurred when I was in high school. I had gone with some amateur (ham) radio friends to a "field day" operation on a local hilltop. I had planned to participate in this event for some time with my parent's approval only to be told at the last minute that I could not go. My parents followed me to the location to bring me home because I had disobeyed their wishes. In the presence of a group of my friends, my mother began to rant and rave about how ungrateful I was and how disobedient I was. She declared that I was not allowed to participate in these activities because of my disobedience. She demanded that I get in the car and leave with them. I got in the car, and as we drove down the hill and out the access road onto the main road, she continued her tirade. I finally got so tired of listening to her that I opened the door and jumped out of the car. The car was traveling at over thirty-five miles an hour at the time. As I rolled out onto the shoulder of the road, I scraped and bruised my shoulder and side pretty severely. But I got up and ran off into the woods.

That startled my parents, and it was several hours before they found me. I had made my way through the woods, back up the hillside to the ham radio group's location, and was with them again when my parents found me. When they again told me I had to go home with them, I went along willingly because I was pretty sore and needed a bandage on my shoulder.

I survived high school and dated some, but I felt awkward dating girls. So, after graduating, I decided to enter the Catholic order of teaching men, the same order of the Christian Brothers who had taught me in high school. They had a novitiate in Rhode Island. I must admit that an element of this decision was the hope that this experience would "cure" me of my gender confusion. This attempt to use religion as an avenue to eliminate my gender confusion became a pattern that I was to follow for the early part of my life. I felt that God would help me find a solution to this turmoil if I was a good person and a devout Christian.

I spent the summer of 1960 in the novitiate. Before the end of the summer, I realized that the contemplative life was not for me, and I left. I had been accepted at a university in Boston and began college there in the fall of 1960. After the restrictive home environment that I grew up in and following my recent experience in the cloistered seminary, the openness of the secular university created the ideal environment for me to cut loose. I did a lot of partying. As a result, I failed almost all of my first-semester classes. After a meeting with the dean of students, we agreed that the university and I would part company. After that, I tried various things, among which was the military. I took the military exams, and I scored high marks on all of them. The Navy offered to send me to electronics school, which was right up my alley, so I decided to join.

My Navy Years and Meeting the "Love of My Life"

Jan and I met when we were both teenagers. I was eighteen, and Jan had just turned sixteen. After being asked to leave the university in the winter of 1960, I joined the Navy on February 14, 1961. I was sent to boot camp at the Great Lakes Naval Training Center in Illinois, north of Chicago. Since I had experience as a member of the Army ROTC Drill Team at the university, I was assigned to Drill Company 5909 and began training on February 27, 1961. I graduated from boot camp on May 1, 1961. After returning home to Massachusetts for a short leave, I was sent back to Great Lakes to await my Electronics Technician Class "A" training school there, which was due to start in early June.

While I waited for the school to start, I was assigned to what the Navy called "mess" duty, which involved serving food on the chow line, cleaning the chow halls, cleaning the trays, utensils, etc., and assisting the cooks with the preparation of the food. Other sailors awaiting the commencement of various training schools were assigned by the Navy to similar duties following boot camp or other assignments. Since we were together for a short period, we developed a few friendships.

One of the young men whom I was hanging around with was a sailor assigned to this duty following his release from the Navy brig. He was from the Chicago area and invited me to visit his family in Cicero on liberty. He was a rough character—friendly, but a tough person. He showed me around the Chicago area and took me to a tattoo parlor in a shady area of Chicago. I wasn't interested in getting any tattoos. Apparently, some members of his family were associated with the Chicago mob. He assured me that if I wanted to get rid of anybody, he could find one of his relatives to take care of whoever was bothering me. It was clear that going down that road would not lead to the same kind of life I lived in Massachusetts. It was likely that I would be associating with a rougher community and skirting the edges of legality.

I met another young sailor one day while serving on the chow line together. Ron and I became lifelong friends. We used to joke that when we met, one of us was serving peas, and the other was serving mashed potatoes. We were walking together to the movie theater on base one evening with several other sailors from the barracks, and he was talking about visiting his family. He showed me a picture of his sister and invited me to come with him to visit his family in Northwestern Ohio. This incident began our travels together from Great Lakes to the Northwestern Ohio area on weekend liberty. His hometown, Findlay, Ohio, was just about at the limit of how far we were allowed to go on weekend liberty from Great Lakes.

I began dating Ron's sister, Pat, who had experienced some disagreements with her mother and was grounded. The family rule, someone told me, was that the only time she could go on a date was when she double-dated with her brother. Since I was with him, she was dating me. Unfortunately, her boyfriend objected to that arrangement, so eventually it was going to end. One weekend in June 1961, when we arrived at Ron's house on Friday evening, another girl was there. Ron told me that this girl, Jan, was Pat's best friend, and she was there to spend the weekend with her. I was irritated, feeling that Jan would be occupying Pat's time and that I wouldn't have any time with her. I found out later that Jan had similar feelings of irritation. She thought that I would be occupying Pat's time and that she would not be able to spend as much time with her best friend.

However, during the day Saturday, Jan and I got to spend some time together. We learned that we liked each other and being together, and by evening time we had concluded that we were happier with each other than with Pat. I learned later from Jan that she told Pat that night that she planned to marry me. Later, we found out that Pat's and Jan's mothers arranged the weekend. They worked together at a local manufacturing plant and had come up with the plan to reconcile Pat and her boyfriend, who was now back in good graces with Pat's mom.

We spent most of that weekend together, and our affection for each other grew rapidly. When I returned to Great Lakes, I wrote her a long letter, and she returned a long letter to me. That began several months of letters going back and forth between Jan's house in Ohio and my barracks in Great Lakes. Jan and I went on a lot of fun dates in Ohio. I remember July 4 was a particularly enjoyable time. Because both of us were young and inexperienced in matters of love, we were not engaging in any serious physical activity other than kissing and hugging and so forth. We were both pretty much what you call prudes, although Jan was stronger than I was, and she was adamant that there was no way that we were going to go "all the way."

I completed my electronics training school in mid-December of 1961, and the Navy assigned me to a ship stationed in

Norfolk, Virginia, the USS *Oxford* (AG–159), a technical research ship. When I left Great Lakes, I had two weeks' leave available before boarding the *Oxford*, so I stopped at Jan's house in Ohio and planned to spend those two weeks there. While I was there, I got a call from my parents. The Navy notified them that my ship was due to leave Norfolk on a cruise. I needed to be on board before they left. Jan's family put me on a train to Norfolk, and I arrived just in time to report in.

USS Oxford (AG-159) [2]

The *Oxford* left Norfolk on January 4, 1962, for South America. On the cruise, we visited (in order) the ports of Colón, Panama; Recife and Santos, Brazil (the port city for São Paulo); Montevideo, Uruguay; Buenos Aires, Argentina; Rio de Janeiro, Brazil; and San Juan, Puerto Rico. In the

---

[2] https://en.wikipedia.org/wiki/USS_Oxford_(AGTR-1)

process, we crossed the equator twice. The first occurred on February 1, 1962. The event was commemorated with the traditional sailors' line-crossing ceremony, in which I, a lowly pollywog, was initiated by King Neptune and became a trusty shellback.

The ship's stopover for liberty in Santos, Brazil, was the occasion for a life lesson that was forever burned into my memory. Two of my shipboard friends had decided that I needed to go on liberty and raise "hell." I had very little experience with drinking alcohol, and they decided we would go to the Santos beach and get some alcohol and get drunk. When we reached the beach, we went to the beach house and changed out of our uniforms and into swimsuits. They then decided they'd go on the prowl to pick up some girls to party with us. They left me alone on the beach to guard our clothes, especially the liquor we purchased. I sat there for some time, awaiting their return. Finally, I decided to start drinking some of the rum they had purchased. By the time they returned (without any girls), I had just about consumed the whole bottle of rum and was roaring drunk. They decided that I needed to return to the ship and that we needed to change back into our uniforms. I apparently decided the best place to do that was in the middle of the road adjacent to the beach. So, they told me that I undressed and put on my uniform in the middle of the main road of Santos. Fortunately, it was late at night, and we didn't run into any police.

When we returned to the ship, they had a major problem with me. I needed to get down the steep, narrow ship's ladder to the berthing compartment. I was so drunk that my "friends" just got me to the top of the ladder and shoved me. I tumbled down the ladder in a drunken stupor and landed there bruised and battered but with no broken bones. That incident resulted in my explaining to the ship's captain why I was in that condition. From that time, my experience with alcohol has been very limited, and the smell of rum makes me ill. Lesson learned!

One of the other exciting experiences of *Oxford*'s South American cruise was that, as a research ship, *Oxford* participated in Naval Research Laboratories' experiments. These involved moon-bounce communications (bouncing a signal from the Earth to the moon and back to the Earth). On March 30, 1962, the *Oxford* was the first ship to communicate from the sea to a shore station utilizing moon relay.

> *During the next two years, the Communication Moon Relay system expanded to include ship-to-shore communications. A sixteen-foot (five-meter), steerable parabolic antenna and receiving equipment installed on the USS Oxford in 1961 permitted one-way shore-to-ship lunar satellite communications for the first time. The addition of a one-kilowatt transmitter to the Oxford in 1962 permitted two-way communications as the ship sailed in South American waters. These successful trial experiments with the USS Oxford led to the establishment of the Navy's worldwide artificial satellite communications system later in the decade.*[3]

The message received on the *Oxford* by moon bounce follows:

> *This communication from the US Naval Research Laboratory at Washington, DC, to the USS Oxford at sea using UHF radio via the moon-bounce path marks a significant new first in radio The laboratory is proud of its many great contributions to radio communications over the years and is pleased to welcome the USS Oxford to the large family of naval vessels which has participated significantly in the Navy's Radio Communication Research Program.*
>
> *(Signed) RM Page*
> *Director of Research*[4]

---

[3] https://history.nasa.gov/SP-4217/ch2.htm

[4] *Naval Research Reviews*, February 1962, p. 22.

This experimentation was a precursor to today's satellite communications. Space for the naval research equipment was assigned next to the electronics shop where I worked. So, I could observe their experiments. The sixteen-foot dish antenna they used for their moon-relay communications was mounted directly above our spaces on the ship's fantail. We often heard the whirring of the antennas' motors as they tracked the moon's position while the ship moved through the ocean.

In May of 1962, with the *Oxford* back in Norfolk from South America, I drove to Ohio, took Jan to her junior prom, and gave her an engagement ring. We had decided that we were going to get married.

Jan's junior prom, 1962, with Ted

In August 1962, *Oxford* left Norfolk with an assignment to monitor communications activity in the Caribbean area around Cuba. While I was on the ship on its way to Cuba, Jan's mother found out about the engagement ring and insisted that she return it to me. Since I was at sea, Jan decided to send it back to the jeweler where I purchased it. I got a letter from her telling me that she had returned the ring and that her mother had demanded that we stop seeing each other. We wrote back and forth and decided that there was some sense in her mother's decision since Jan was still in school and I would be on the ship for a lengthy cruise.

The *Oxford* was critical in monitoring communications between Cuba and Russia and played a significant role in gathering intelligence leading up to and during the Cuban Missile Crisis of October 1962. The website *StationHypo.com* gives a summary of *Oxford*'s involvement in the crisis:

> The Center for Cryptologic History's Almanac 50th Anniversary series article, "The TRS Program Part I: The Beginning," describes perfectly the Oxford's significant contribution to the Cuban Missile Crisis.

> The Oxford was officially known as a technical research ship. Its initial mission was a training cruise. This gave the crew a chance to familiarize themselves with equipment on board and to identify any problems with the newly refurbished, redesigned ship before traveling to the Middle East. Although several features were identified that required change or improvement, overall, the test proved to be a great success. For example, the Oxford recorded frequencies and collected a large number of other transmissions. As the capabilities of the Oxford became clear, the list of potential targets for these ships quickly expanded to include countries all over the globe.

> In August 1962, as relations between the United States and the Soviet Union over Cuba grew increasingly tense, the Oxford was diverted to the Caribbean. Its mission was to collect the communications coming out of Cuba, used by both Soviet and Cuban

entities. The Oxford proved to be the largest producer of SIGINT[5] during the Cuban Missile Crisis [emphasis added]. The communications it collected provided a great quantity of information which, when combined with the photographs from the U2 overflights, provided a very good picture of what was happening in Cuba.

USS Oxford's success in the Cuban Missile Crisis "demonstrated the value of the TRS program" and paved the way for naval cryptology aboard future technical research ships: Georgetown, Jamestown, Muller, Belmont, and Liberty.[6,7]

The *Oxford* became a thorn in Castro's side, and he made several attempts to drive the ship from the Cuban vicinity. Several times he sent gunboats to threaten to sink the ship, and the *Oxford*'s limited armament provided little defensive capabilities. According to a newspaper article that one of my shipmates received from home, Castro had complained to the UN, noting our presence and requesting that the UN demand our removal. When President Kennedy announced to the nation the Cuban crisis, with missiles received from Russia, the *Oxford* was on station in sight of Havana harbor.

During this time frame, I decided to apply for the Navy's Nuclear Power School to prepare to operate nuclear reactors on Navy surface ships. When *Oxford* returned to Norfolk,

---

[5] Signals Intelligence

[6] Not listed was the USS Pueblo, which was captured by the North Korean Navy on January 23, 1968. For more information on technical research ships in general, and the USS Liberty in particular, see Scott, James (2009), The Attack on the Liberty: The Untold Story of Israel's Deadly 1967 Assault on a US Spy Ship, Simon and Schuster, ISBN 978-1-4165-5482-0.

[7] https://stationhypo.com/2015/11/25/uss-oxford-the-largest-producer-of-sigint-in-the-cuban-missile-crisis/ and The_TRS_Program:_Part_I.pdf at nsa.gov

I received the assignment to the nuclear power training facility in Bainbridge, Maryland. The course was an intensive six-month classroom training program that outlined naval nuclear power plants' construction and operational principles. After graduation from that preliminary program, I was assigned operational training at the Navy's nuclear power training facility in Upstate New York outside of Ballston Spa in West Milton. This facility, known as the Knolls Atomic Power Laboratory, had two fully operational Navy nuclear reactors. One was a submarine reactor system, and the other was a surface ship reactor system similar to one of the reactors on the carrier USS *Enterprise.*

This portion of the training was an intense experience similar to boot camp. We were required to know the operation of all the elements of the reactor system, including the piping, valves, electrical systems, and electronic controls. I was to be a reactor control operator, so I would not be required to maintain piping systems and so forth. In any case, all personnel were required to be familiar with the entire plant. In an emergency, any sailor needed to be precise in reporting the nature and location of the incident. Also, they must be able to perform any remedial steps that would be required. It was common for sailors passing through the plant to be called to attention by an instructor. They were then required to detail the characteristics and operation of nearby portions of the plant. We were all required to stand at attention and recite the fluid type in each pipe (plain or radioactive water) and the manufacturer and operational statistics of each pipe, valve, and controller in the facility. It seemed as if the instructors took unique joy in tripping us up and then criticizing us mercilessly for our lack of knowledge. Because of the intensity of the training environment, as well as other issues, I experienced an emotional breakdown.

I had a couple of friends I was hanging around with who were quite actively partying and dating, and I felt conflicted and left out. One weekend I went along with these two friends to Long Island to stay with a friend of one of my buddies. I found out that the "friend" was a married ex-girl-friend of one of these two. That night while we were sleeping downstairs, I was awakened by the sound of a rifle being cocked. Apparently, the girl's husband had come home, and he decided that one of us had been sleeping with his wife. He determined that he would shoot whichever of us was the culprit and that if we didn't talk, he would kill all of us. The friend who had arranged this stopover and the wife assured the angry husband that there had been nothing wrong with our visit and talked him out of shooting any of us. We left immediately, and I felt that I had escaped a very scary situation. I found out later that the person who arranged the visit actually was sleeping with the wife and had put us in that dangerous situation.

Another cause of my breakdown was continuing gender conflict. This conflict had been a part of my life since I was a child, but I had never eliminated those feelings. One morning at breakfast, my two friends talked about their dates and made fun of me since I had not been dating. I got so mad that I drove a knife through my plate and into the table. The plate shattered and cut my hand deeply. I went to the base corpsman to get stitched up, and he questioned me about the accident. He decided to have me evaluated to see if I was emotionally fit to be a reactor control operator. Before completing the training, I was sent to the St. Albans (Queens, New York) Naval Hospital for evaluation and dropped from the nuclear power program.

From there, I went to the Brooklyn Navy Yard for reassign-ment. I was later assigned to the cryptographic equipment school in Norfolk, Virginia.

I don't remember whether Jan caught up to me in Brooklyn or Norfolk, but she had decided that we needed to get back together. After graduating from high school, she worked at the manufacturing plant near her home, where her mother and stepfather worked. Jan told me that she took change to work every day and spent each lunch hour in the phone booth, calling various Navy facilities and trying to track me down. She was finally successful, and we got back together again. I began visiting her in Ohio at regular intervals.

When I completed the crypto school in Norfolk, I was assigned to a minesweeper, the USS *Skill* (MSO-471), with a home port in Charleston, South Carolina. The *Skill* was a wooden-hull (nonmagnetic) ocean-going minesweeper designed to disable various types of mines (mostly magnetic and acoustic types) that enemies would place in shipping lanes. I was assigned as an electronics technician tasked with maintaining and repairing various shipboard communications equipment.

USS Skill *(MSO-471)*[8]

---

[8] http://www.navsource.org/archives/11/110247107.jpg

On board, I became good friends with a couple of brothers from Kannapolis, North Carolina. Since Kannapolis was relatively close to Charleston, we would often drive up there on liberty. One weekend I purchased a red 1962 Ford Galaxie 500 at a Ford dealer there in Kannapolis. That was a car that I remember to this day. I took that car on many trips to Ohio from Charleston. In the front seat of that Ford, I asked Jan to marry me for the second time.

Jan and I had many discussions about how, when, and where we would get married. Since her mother had previously opposed our marriage, it was not surprising when she opposed it this time. Jan and her mother had several discussions about our impending marriage, and her mother was unalterably opposed. Jan and I decided that it would be legal for us to marry in South Carolina without her mother's permission. I would send her the money to purchase a bus or train ticket to Charleston, and we would be married there. When Jan told her mother that this was our plan, her mother burst into tears and asked Jan how she could do that. She told Jan she wanted to have a shower for her and to celebrate the wedding with us. This abrupt turnaround was surprising, but we decided it would be better to have the wedding there in Ohio with her mother's permission.

To save up money for the wedding, I sold my beloved '62 Ford, and we planned to drive the Rambler that Jan owned. We were married in a little country church, literally in a wide spot in the road, in Eagleville, Ohio, on Saturday, November 28, 1964. Present were mostly Jan's relatives and some of our friends. It was a forgone conclusion among most of the attendees that the marriage wouldn't last. We had too much against us. I was a sailor from Massachusetts and had been raised Catholic. Jan was a farm girl from Ohio and had been raised in the Pentecostal Church. Her grandfather was a

Pentecostal preacher, and her whole family were dedicated Pentecostal Church members. We just had too many strikes against us. Little did they know that we would overcome many obstacles, and the marriage would last almost fifty-five years.

Ted and Jan's wedding portrait, November 28, 1964

We spent our wedding night in the Continental Inn in Toledo. That night we spent watching *Gunsmoke* on television and talking. Jan had told me previously that she had experienced abuse by some of her mother's male friends as a child and was very afraid to engage in any intimate activities. So, our wedding night was very quiet.

The next day (Sunday), we drove back to Jan's mother's home, gathered her belongings, and headed out for our "honeymoon." That was a trip to my parents' home in Massachusetts and then on to Charleston, where I had rented us a small home. On the way, Jan's old Rambler developed engine problems in a snowstorm outside of Erie, Pennsylvania. We got a tow truck to come and get us off the road, and they dropped us off at a motel on Route 19 near the highway. The next morning, we walked across the road to a donut shop for breakfast. Unfortunately, when it came time to pay our bill, I discovered that I had left my wallet in the motel room. I left Jan as "collateral" to guarantee my return. The donut shop owners figured that it was a good bet I'd be back since we were newlyweds. That incident remained one of those little experiences in life that we laughed at many times later.

We had Jan's car towed to a local motorcycle repair shop that agreed to look at it. They determined that the engine had valve problems. A couple of days later, and with a large bite out of our savings, we were back on our way to Massachusetts. We stayed in a motel in Waltham while we visited my parents. The visit didn't go well. My mother was nasty to Jan. She declared that since we were not married in the Catholic Church, we were living in sin and that Jan had made me leave the church to marry her.

One of our plans had been to retrieve a 1957 Mercury Monterey that I had purchased when I was in Ballston Spa at Nuclear Power School. I had left it with my parents after St. Albans, on the way to being reassigned. I planned to drive it to Charleston and use it there. My father could not find the keys for the Mercury, and the visit was altogether unpleasant, so we decided to head to Charleston and leave the car there. I understood later that my father called a junkyard and had it hauled away. That was disappointing since my friends in New York and I had done considerable work on it, and it was quite a speedy vehicle.

Jan and I drove on to Charleston and got settled in our house there in North Charleston. It was a few months later when we decided to get a new turquoise 1964 Ford Falcon. It was a nice, reliable little car that we kept for several years after I got out of the Navy.

Jan's Story

The following was written by Jan in 2014 and 2016.

I was born on February 17, 1945, in Fort Wayne, Indiana. At that time, my father was an engineer at radio station WOWO in Fort Wayne. Later we moved for a short time to South Carolina, and then in 1948, we moved to Findlay, Ohio, and lived on Central Avenue, upstairs from the Church of God and across the street from Lucy's family store. About 1950, we moved to a house trailer in a side lot on Carnahan; the trailer was owned by an older gentleman.

My parents registered me for kindergarten at the old McKee School on Tiffin Avenue in Findlay. I started kindergarten in September 1950 at the McKinley Grade School on Lynn Street. The family attended the Church of God on Main Street. In 1952, we moved to our first house on Carnahan Avenue in Findlay.

In 1953 my mom and dad divorced,[9] and Mom started work at an area manufacturing plant in September. In 1954

---

[9] Jan's parents' divorce was brought on by fighting between her parents. One or the other would start a fight when Jan was in bed, and Jan would be awakened to mediate the battle. She lived in fear that one of her parents would be killed and it would be her fault for not being a "good enough" daughter.

Mom married a family friend and widower from our church. He was from the farming community of Cygnet, north of Findlay. I first experienced sexual assault from him. I never told my mom about the assault. About 1956, Mom divorced him.

In 1957 Mom remarried (he also worked at the plant she did). Mom sold the house in Findlay, and we moved to her new husband's farm in Bloomdale, Ohio. I started seventh grade at Bloomdale School in September. My stepbrother Jeff was born in October 1957. Two other stepsiblings were born in quick succession. My stepsister Jody was born in October 1958, and my stepbrother Thomas was born in December 1959. In 1962 my stepsister Lesa was born in February, rounding out the family.[10]

In 1961 I met and started dating Ted on the last weekend in June. I was staying the weekend with my best friend, Pat. Our mothers were in cahoots to set me up with Ted, a Navy friend of Pat's brother, Ron. Ted spent the weekends with Pat's family. Neither Ted nor I knew about the fix-up. We hit it off, and over the next three weeks till his next weekend off, we corresponded almost daily.

In May of 1962, Ted went with me to the junior prom. He gave me an engagement ring. Mom made me send it back to the jeweler in New York when Ted was on a Navy cruise to the Caribbean area. Ted and I decided to split up then. In 1963 a friend from school asked me to the senior prom. In June, I graduated from Elmwood High School and, in July, started work on the second shift at the plant where Mom and my stepfather worked.

---

[10] One of the problems of being a teenager with four young stepsiblings was that Jan became a built-in babysitter. Her mother returned to work in the plant in Findlay, leaving Jan to babysit on a regular basis for no payment.

In 1964 Ted and I were married. Ironically, when we repeated our vows, the pastor said to me, "I, Janice, take thee, Edward, to be my lawful wedded wife." I corrected it, of course. Maybe he knew something I didn't.

Part of the "baggage" I brought to the marriage was my upbringing in an ultraconservative, religious family. I learned early to merely tolerate people of different religious, ethnic, and economic backgrounds. If someone didn't believe as our family did, we thought they were simply confused. So, when I married a "sailor" who was also a Catholic from New England, my family essentially wrote me off and said our marriage wouldn't last more than six months.

The Navy scheduled Ted's ship to go on a six-week Navy cruise in May 1965. I decided to go home to Ohio. When they canceled the cruise, I returned to Charleston. We were planning to go out to dinner one evening shortly after my return, and I went to put on my favorite skirt and noticed that the zipper was broken. I knew it was okay the last time I wore it. Since I was still a new wife and lacked self-confidence, I immediately thought Ted must have found another woman while I was gone. Little did I know that the "other woman" was my husband.

Ted said, "Honey, we need to talk." Those words changed my life. He told me that the zipper broke when he wore the skirt. We had a long discussion that night, and he told me that he liked to wear women's clothes; it was a stress reliever. It was a difficult night for both of us, as he feared that I'd leave him. I assured him that I meant those vows I had taken, and we'd get through this together. Thus began the first of many discussions about his secret life.

We agreed to keep this information just between us and deal with it as it came up. For several years after that, Ted would dress in women's clothing whenever he was under much stress. I wouldn't say I liked it, but I knew we could have worse problems. At least he wasn't physically abusing me. We attended couple's counseling with a Christian therapist as we both struggled with this perceived "sin."

Over the next few years, we discussed the issue at length. Sometimes it seemed all we talked about was that. Other times we'd not mention it for months. I hoped it would go away if we ignored it.

When our son was born in 1968, we thought perhaps parenthood would solve the "problem." It didn't, of course. As our son grew, we struggled with telling him so that he would not walk in sometime and find his father cross-dressed. We decided to wait until he graduated from high school.

We moved to the Boston area in 1983 to take care of Ted's parents, who were in ill health. His father died in May of 1983, we moved to his parents' home in Waltham in August of that year, and his mother died in a Waltham nursing home in October of 1983. We moved to Wilmington, Massachusetts, in December of 1983.

One day in 1983, while we were still living in his parents' Waltham home, Ted called an area help line looking for support in dealing with his cross-dressing. They sent us to a local support group, the Tiffany Club, located in Wayland, Massachusetts. I discovered there that I wasn't the only wife whose husband was a cross-dresser. My first experience outside the home was driving to a mall parking lot late at night and walking with Diane around the mall. Our involvement with Tiffany Club went from dinner with some other cross-dressed couples, to writing and editing the monthly support-group newsletter and magazine, to cross-dressing conventions.

In the early '90s, as the journey progressed, we felt we had outgrown the Tiffany Club, and in 1999, after many years of counseling for both of us, Diane determined she was not a cross-dresser, but that she was actually transsexual. As we were nearing Y2K and Diane was nearing age sixty, she decided to begin the transition from male to female, saying, "If not now, when?"

Around 1988 we had revealed to our son Diane's cross-dressing. He said he didn't approve. Diane told him she didn't need his approval; he has struggled with Diane's gender identity since. One thing about "coming out" to other people is that you never can anticipate their reactions. In 2000, when we told our son that Ted was transitioning, he again voiced his disapproval, but we told him that it was a life-and-death decision. He was very hesitant about telling his wife, and it was a year or so before he decided that we could discuss the issue with her. We decided dinner at their home was the best setting. Our daughter-in-law's first question to Diane was when could they go shopping for jewelry together. Diane's relationship with our son seems to have improved over the years, but it's still difficult for our son.

The Harry Benjamin Standard of Care at that time recommended that the transitioning person live for one year in the gender of their choice before surgery could be done. In 2000 she began the transition process, taking hormones, and in 2001, after being laid off, she began living full-time as a female, legally changing her name and driver's license in July 2001. One of the most difficult and emotional changes for me was when she had her ears pierced. I had become somewhat used to her dressing as a female, but getting her ears pierced was the one thing I had left that was mine alone.

I felt sure then that I had lost my husband. It was really difficult emotionally.

When we decided that Ted would transition to live as Diane, we both felt the need to become involved in a local church. We found that church in the Ballard Vale United Church in Andover, Massachusetts. We became active in Bible study, choir, and other areas. Our faith grew over the years, and we both became more tolerant of people's differences.

One thing that has allowed me to accept this aspect of our lives is knowing that this is a physical issue and not something she can choose. It's rather like being left-handed or having blue eyes.

Diane had struggled most of her life and was finally going to become the woman she felt she truly was. With all the changes happening, I needed to get something out of this process too. I never had an extensive wardrobe, so we made an agreement on clothing. Whenever Diane got new clothes or jewelry, I could spend up to twice as much on my wardrobe. Nothing extravagant for either of us, but it helped me handle the stress somewhat better. All male-to-female persons transitioning seem to have favorite parts of their appearances. For some, it's clothes; some love getting manicures; some it's jewelry. I'm just thankful that she never went through the flamboyant stage. I do have to share my chocolate with her now, though. Ted never cared much for chocolates, not so with Diane.

As I said before, "coming out" to other people is never easy. You never really know what their reactions will be. When I told my mom and sister, it was a different situation. Mom is ultraconservative and didn't accept it at all, even though Diane and I had been married nearly forty years. Her reaction was that she didn't want "that person" to attend her funeral.

My sister also didn't understand, but decided to research the Internet. Mom has now accepted Diane, though I have several family members we don't see very often and don't know about her.

Security and privacy in the workplace are major factors for spouses and the trans person. Employees chat about family activities at lunch and around the water cooler. I was always cautious about using the correct pronouns when referring to Ted. It was like a balancing act. I had only two colleagues who became good enough friends that I felt comfortable "coming out" to. Finally, I learned the safest way to discuss family was to simply use "we."

Since her transition, I've accompanied Diane to several events, church conventions, and college classes. So, in some way, I guess I've "come a long way, baby." Yes, I still miss my husband, and there are things that I still wouldn't feel comfortable doing, such as strolling down the beach hand-in-hand or ballroom dancing, something about which I'd always fantasized. However, I still have this person with me. The one who has stood by me through having a son stillborn, through the most aggressive type of breast cancer (chemo, surgery, and radiation over fourteen months), and through total knee replacement and recovery. We renewed our wedding vows in November 2014, and we still believe "till death do us part." Diane is the one person I can always count on to be there when I need her.

It's been a long road; some days are easier than others. Our relationship has changed from spouse to partner, even though we're still legally married. After fifty years and counting, as of today, I still believe those vows to "love, honor, and cherish, so long as we both shall live." I'm proud to say that we have a wonderful son, daughter-in-law, and two beautiful grandchildren.

Living with Gender Identity Issues

In the words of that famous American philosopher Kermit the Frog, "It's not easy bein' green." Kermit's point was that he blended in with the background of green leaves and "so many other ordinary things." Beginning in the '70s, generations of children have heard and understood Kermit's message about the difficulty of being uncomfortable with your true self. By the end of his little song, though, Kermit admits, "I am green, and it'll do fine. It's beautiful! And I think it's what I want to be."

Every trans person I've known—and I've known hundreds, if not thousands—has struggled with their gender identity from early childhood. Most of the time, they and their parents couldn't identify the issues related to gender identity. Still, as they grew older and as more information became available, they recognized the markers that had been there throughout their lives.

From as far back as I can remember, I've known that I wasn't the same as other boys and girls. As I grew up in the '40s and '50s, I remember that my parents told me repeatedly that I needed to "act like a boy!" Obviously, I was doing something, even as a preschooler that projected my feelings that I was a girl. But I learned. I learned to "act like a boy."

It's not really "acting" though. It's hiding the things about yourself that you don't understand and that society doesn't accept. It's protecting yourself from society's critical eye so that you can live a life as uncomplicated and peaceful as possible. One of the criticisms I heard from Jan and other family members of trans people is that "they've/you've been living a lie." It's not lying. It's self-protection. In the self-confusion of gender identity, while you are still trying to figure out where you fit in, it's easiest not to reveal your struggles to everyone. As one counselor suggested, we need to ask ourselves, "Does this person need to know about my struggles?" For many of our coworkers, acquaintances, and family members, the answer is no. Even revealing those issues to close family members and spouses becomes difficult. Will they accept us…or reject and abandon us?

That was the question I had when I married Jan and, later in life, when our son was old enough to be told. With Jan, that episode with the broken zipper on her favorite skirt, which Jan mentioned earlier, prompted the discussion as a means to allay her suspicions. The broken zipper indicated to Jan that another woman had worn the skirt. I could not have her think that I had been unfaithful. Revealing my gender confusion and cross-dressing was the lesser of two evils. No matter how risky the gender revelation would be, nothing could be worse than having her think I had been unfaithful to her.

It's really hard to describe what gender confusion is all about. I suppose it's like trying to describe color to a blind person. If you haven't experienced it, it's hard to grasp the concept. For most persons whose perception of their gender matches their physical characteristics (*cis* or *cisgender*), the concept of being unsure about their gender is completely foreign. The usual description of "a woman trapped in a man's body" doesn't really do justice to the level of confusion I experienced and what I've observed in others like me. That description isn't even very accurate since we are not trapped in the wrong body. We are trapped in a society that forces everyone to fit into one of two (*binary gender*) patterns deemed acceptable to the majority. As a result, I felt as if my life was "out of sync" with society.

A good description of the emotional conflict is that it is like the sound-picture synchronization of a movie. For most persons, their gender perception and their sexual characteristics are "in sync." For cisgender persons, their lives progress without any confusion or conflict between the two parts. For most transgender persons like me, however, it is as if the "sound" part of my life didn't match the "picture" part of my life. When you watch a movie that has sound out of sync with the picture, it requires intense concentration to try to match the two elements so that you can make sense out of the story. Similarly, matching your own gender-sex elements when they are out of sync requires a great deal of concentration. I went through life constantly tense—trying to force those elements into sync. Daily life became a constant effort to force those two parts to come together.

For most of us who struggle with this issue, we come to a point in our lives when we can no longer manage the tension. That's when it comes down to the most basic of choices—life or death—a life that involves gender transition to resolve the conflict, or death. Unfortunately, too many of us find the latter—ending our lives—the easier choice. Those who say that gender transition is a choice do not understand the true conflict. The choice is not to be transgender or not. The choice is between life and death, between suicide or transitioning so that your gender-sex conflict is resolved by matching the physical sex characteristics to your gender perception.

I was about ten years old when Christine Jorgensen returned to the US in 1953, following her gender transition in Denmark. I remember the feeling I first had that my dreams of becoming a girl were not hopeless. I could do what she had done to become a girl. Then, the feeling of despair came when I heard the derisive comments and jokes made about Christine in the media and by my family and friends. As much as I wanted to be a girl, I thought then that it was something I would never be able to do.

My teenage years were horrible. It's hard enough for the average teenager to figure out the boy-girl relationship, but it was impossible for someone like me. I wasn't sure who I was. How could I figure out my relationship with other boys or girls? If I was a boy, was I gay and attracted to boys? If I was a girl, was I gay if I was attracted to girls?

So, I played my part and "acted like a man." I figured that all this confusion came from the fact that I'd never had a relationship with a girl and that when I found the right woman and got married, it would all go away. Then I met Jan, and we fell in love. I wasn't acting; I really fell in love. We were married in the midsixties, and I was sure all the gender confusion was in my past.

What happened was exactly the opposite. We were together constantly, and I was intimately involved with a woman. I was learning what a woman's life was really like. Instead of the gender confusion diminishing, it increased exponentially. I thought I was going crazy. Finally, about six months after our wedding, the skirt incident occurred, and it forced the issue. I told Jan that I had worn some of her clothes, and we talked about what was going on. We decided that our love for each other was strong enough to overcome or survive this challenge.

As I said, I thought I was going crazy. I decided to talk to a Navy psychiatrist to figure out what was going on. I requested that our ship's corpsman get me an appointment with the Navy hospital psychiatrist. He admitted me to Charleston Naval Hospital for observation. Eventually, at the direction of the doctors there, I was discharged from the Navy. My discharge was honorable due to "physical disability." The psychiatrist's evaluation was that I was not suitable for Navy service because I was too dependent on the females in my life, namely my mother and my wife.

In the midsixties we became members of an independent Fundamentalist Christian Church. I dedicated my life to Christ. I believed Jesus's words: "I tell you the truth, if you have faith as small as a mustard seed, you can say to this mountain, 'Move from here to there,' and it will move. Nothing will be impossible for you" (Matthew 17:20). My situation surely wasn't as hard as moving a mountain, so I felt that what I needed was to strengthen my faith, and it would all go away.

I became a pastor, attended seminary in Cincinnati, and ministered to several churches. It didn't go away.

By the late '70s I was really confused. Nothing was helping to diminish those feelings. Jan was frustrated. We had a son who needed me as his father. We decided that we needed help, so we spoke to a Christian counselor who was a member of our church. After several sessions, I finally broke down and revealed to him my feelings of confusion about my gender. Surprisingly, he didn't shake the Bible at me and declare me a sinner. He told me that I must stop worrying, that God loved me, regardless of my feelings, and that I just needed to learn what God wanted me to do. As I began to pray—not that it be removed from my life, but for wisdom to know how to handle it—I began to find the beginnings of peace.

In the early '80s we moved from Cincinnati to Massachusetts. One day, as despair began to creep back into my life, I called a help line. They referred me to a support group for "transvestites." That call began our education about what was really happening in my life. As Jan and I interacted with males and females struggling with their gender identity, and with the spouses of these transgender persons, we learned where we fit in. I began to understand more about what was happening in my life and learned that it wasn't ever "going away."

By the late '80s we had integrated my transgender experience into our lives. I was satisfied, at this point, to express my gender identity through cross-dressing. I could not admit, even to myself yet, that I was transsexual, that I needed to transition to live as my true self. I knew too many friends who had transitioned and had lost everything—family, friends, jobs…everything.

We were active in the local transgender support group and an Evangelical Church in Massachusetts—careful not to mix the two. We were uncomfortable, though, with our "secret." We held various positions in the church. I was a member of the board of directors of the transgender support group, and Jan and I edited their monthly newsletter. We also worked with a national transgender organization, editing newsletters and helping in their office. I was a member of the church board and a Bible school teacher, communion leader, and occasional preacher.

Finally, we decided to discuss our transgender life with our pastor, a close friend. I did some personal study and read some articles about the Bible's teachings related to transgender people. I had concluded that there was nothing that I could see that indicated that being transgender was wrong. I also felt that the Bible's discussion of eunuchs indicated that the church should accept transgender persons. I took my conclusions to the pastor. As we discussed this, I asked for his prayerful study of these issues to see if I had missed anything or if anything was wrong with my understanding of the various relevant passages.

After several counseling sessions, I attended a regular meeting of the church board. As the first order of business, the pastor read a lengthy list of the reasons why my activities as a transgender person made me unfit to serve in any official capacity in the church. He then proposed that the board remove me from any current responsibilities and declare me unfit to serve in the future. The board accepted his proposition.

I was devastated. I felt betrayed by my pastor and friend and by others on the board who were my friends. At a time of great turmoil and questioning in my life, I felt that my church had cast me aside. After several months of attempting to resolve the issues with church leaders, we stopped attending church. It was at this point that we were forced to reveal my transgender feelings to our son. We had been so active in the church that cutting off our relationships there required explanation.

He was angry. He felt betrayed by his parents. He believed that we had lied to him about an important part of our lives. We thought we were protecting him from something that we didn't understand ourselves. It was only recently that we had begun to understand that we were not alone in these experiences and that medical science was beginning to understand that gender differences were normal variations in humanity. His anger was not diminished, and our relationship was damaged.

Throughout the '90s we continued to work to understand what God wanted me to do with my life. We had both worked with counselors who specialized in treating transgender clients. I was beginning to realize, for several reasons, that I was not a cross-dresser. I was a transsexual. That idea panicked me. I remembered what happened to Christine Jorgensen and many others I had seen who had made the transition. I knew that there was a very real chance that I would lose Jan and our son, as well as my job and most of my friends.

Finally, in 1999, following my son's graduation from college and his subsequent marriage, I decided it was time to think seriously about beginning to transition to live as a female. Jan and I had several discussions and found a gender counselor who also worked with couples going through this process. In our discussions, we realized that to negotiate this process successfully, we needed to establish a relationship with a supportive church.

I researched and located a church in a neighboring community that was a "federated" or "united" church associated with both the United Church of Christ (UCC) and the United Methodist Church (UMC) denominations. The church also proudly declared that it was "open and affirming" as a UCC congregation and "reconciling" as a UMC congregation. After contacting the church pastor and receiving assurances that they would accept us, we attended regularly. We found them to be a warm and loving community that welcomed us and others of the LGBT community. We were not treated as second-class Christians because I was transsexual. We were welcomed and, as time went on, became involved in various positions in the church.

In July 2001, I went through the legal process of transition. My name change was completed, my driver's license changed, and I began to live as a woman. A few years later, I had surgery that allowed a change to my birth certificate and social security records. A short while after my transition, I realized that the tension that came from feeling out of sync was gone. I was at peace. What a gift!!

Our new church stood by me and prayed for me through my transition and through the two and one-half years of unemployment when I lost my job. They prayed with us about our relationship with our son, who struggled to accept the loss of me as his father and to accept me as a woman. They rejoiced with us as he began the journey back to acceptance and as we began to have more regular access to other family members. They encouraged me as I began to speak at local conferences and national meetings about the need for the church to understand and accept the transgender community as God's blessed children. What a contrast from our other church that rejected us!

Our association with the church led to opportunities for both of us to become more active in the wider church in denominational settings. To do that, we first had to decide which denomination, of the two our church was aligned with, was going to be the one in which we became more involved. I contacted the local UCC conference headquarters and discussed opportunities for my serving as a UCC pastor. I learned that since UCC churches were congregational in structure; each church had a pastor who fit the congregation's own beliefs. Although the UCC is an "open and affirming" denomination, each church was free to prioritize how they would accept diversity. I was told that the likelihood of my getting a preaching ministry as a transgender female was very slim.

However, that initial local contact resulted in my being directed to a diversity program leader at the denominational headquarters in Cleveland, Ohio. As a result, in 2003, I was invited to serve on an advisory committee working to produce a documentary film about the transgender experience. We met several times with the filmmaker and made suggestions concerning content and direction. I was disappointed when the film was completed because it focused almost entirely on the transition of a female-to-male (F2M) transsexual. It is far easier for a cis person to understand and accept the F2M experience, than for someone to have similar acceptance for an M2F trans person. In today's patriarchal society and church, becoming male is far more acceptable than becoming female. With all of society's restrictions on women, even Jan had difficulty understanding why I would want to transition to female. In the film's planning phase, I had suggested to the filmmaker and the advisory committee that a balanced approach would be more beneficial. Unfortunately, at the first showing of the completed film to the committee, I could not withhold my disappointment and made my concerns known. That was the last meeting I had with the committee.

Jan felt our past history with the Evangelical Churches gave her a closer affinity to the UCC. Hence, she became active in the local UCC conference and was appointed a representative from our church to the conference annual meeting. I decided to focus my activities on the UMC denomination and was also designated a representative to the UMC annual conference. I felt that the structure of the UMC would lend itself to denomination-wide efforts to push for acceptance of sexual orientation and gender identity diversity. I came to understand later that there was a significant traditionalist push in the UMC to overcome all attempts at diversity; this opposition would prevent any hopes for acceptance from coming to fruition. Because of our different emphases, there were a few years when Jan and I were an interdenominational couple, each attending the annual meeting of our respective denomination.

I was encouraged by active members and a former pastor of the church to become a member of the Conference Reconciling Committee. This led to other involvements with a growing LGBT church in Cambridge, Massachusetts, known as Cambridge Welcoming Ministries (CWM), led by a couple of young Boston University School of Theology students. The group began meeting early in 2002 in a UMC church in Cambridge, and Jan and I attended quite often. I became the treasurer until 2004.

I was invited by a member of the Conference Reconciling Committee to participate in some early meetings of an unaffiliated UMC organization, the Church Within a Church Movement (CWACM), which was organized in the early 2000s. CWACM "began as a grassroots response, a church within a church (for some, a resistance movement) to discriminatory, harmful, and oppressive actions of the United Methodist Church (UMC) toward transgender, lesbian, gay, and bisexual people. Rather than try to engage the UMC directly to change the official forty plus year position that still says 'homosexuality is incompatible with Christian teaching,' CWACM chose an alternate path; BE the fully inclusive and just church, now."[11] I attended a meeting in Atlanta; I was moved to tears to find a church group that accepted trans persons and all LGBTQI individuals.

Also, about that time, a group from Affirmation United Methodist met at CWM after one of the Sunday services. I became interested in their mission, which was officially adopted in January 2005 "as an independent voice of lesbian, gay, bisexual, transgender, and queer people. Affirmation radically reclaims the compassionate and transforming gospel of Jesus Christ by relentlessly pursuing full inclusion in

---

[11] "https://www.cwac.us/about-the-movement

the church as we journey with the Spirit in creating God's beloved community."[12] It was attractive to me that the group had been participating in the UMC quadrennial general conferences since 1972 when the "incompatible" language was adopted that "exiled" the LGBT community from active participation in the life of the denomination. I was asked to join the Affirmation Council, and Jan and I attended their quarterly meetings at various locations around the country until 2010 when Jan was diagnosed with cancer.

As a member of the Affirmation Council, I attended the 2004 UMC General Conference (GC) in Pittsburg, Pennsylvania, and the 2008 General Conference in Fort Worth, Texas. In 2004 I worked with the Methodist Fellowship for Social Action (MFSA) to create a database to list the delegates to the General Conference. I prepared a list of delegates that could be contacted for particular legislative items of interest to the Coalition of Reconciling UMC groups. I attended the 2008 GC as the Affirmation female spokesperson, participated in protest activities, and led a news conference relating to anti-transgender legislation that had been proposed.

Perhaps the most important change I have experienced is in understanding my transgender nature. It's not a burden to bear or a problem to overcome. It's not a sin to be forgiven or a flaw to be suppressed. It's a gift from God to be lived with. It's who God wants me to be. Today, instead of praying that this "thorn" (2 Corinthians 12:7) be removed, I rejoice that God has given me the great gift of living in two genders. Like Kermit, I can finally say, "I am transsexual, and it'll do fine. It's beautiful! And I think it's what I want to be."

---

[12] "http://www.umaffirm.org/site/about-us

Our Lives as We Lived with My Gender Identity

Jan and I were children of World War II and the subsequent explosion of prosperity that resulted in the '40s and '50s. We met and married in the early '60s, before the real upheavals of that decade. When the political turmoil of the late '60s arrived, we were involved in establishing our lives together, attending seminary, and welcoming our first child.

Following my discharge from the Navy at the end of October 1965, Jan and I traveled to Northwestern Ohio, where Jan's family lived. We made a stop for several days in Washington, DC, to tour some of the historical sites there. When we arrived in Ohio, we stayed for a while with Jan's mother's family in Northwest Ohio. We finally found a small, second-floor, furnished apartment in Findlay, Ohio. We lived there for a year or so until a new apartment complex opened near us. We purchased some furniture and appliances and moved there.

Jan and I found work in Findlay. After moving to Ohio, my first job was working in a Sylvania TV picture tube plant in Ottawa, Ohio. I was assigned to take the tubes off the line and pack them into boxes. It was a hot, dirty, and tiring job. It also presented some danger. Before the picture tubes came off the line, the final step involved removing all the air in the tubes and then sending them through a furnace that sealed the glass vacuum pipette on the neck of the tubes. In the winter, when some employees might leave the back door open to get ventilation, the heated picture tubes coming out of the furnace and off the line would hit the cold air, and they could explode. The result was a series of exploding picture tubes coming off the line with glass shards flying everywhere until someone could get the door closed. I was interested in finding work in a better environment.

I had put my name in places that seemed like better opportunities using the electronics training I received in the Navy. I got a call from the Ohio Bell Telephone Company early in 1966. I was accepted to begin work in Findlay as a central office main frame installer. I was first assigned to work in another office with an experienced installer. The main frame was the place in the central office where the outside telephone lines terminated. The installation process involved running a pair of wires from the street side of the frame to a connector corresponding with the office equipment assigned to the customer.

When my trainer felt I was ready, I was transferred to the Findlay office near where we lived. Jan was also able to get a job as a telephone operator in the same building. We often worked different shifts since Jan had to work whenever they needed operators. I worked mostly day shifts since I had to work with the outside telephone installers servicing the community. A year or so later, I was sent to the Ohio Bell training facility to learn the operation, maintenance, and troubleshooting of the "No. 5 Crossbar" central office system. This system was one of the first telephone office systems that incorporated touch-tone dialing, and it was the system used in the Findlay office. After several weeks of training there,

I was sent back to Findlay, where I was promoted to the position of central office repairman.

During this time, my friend Ron, who had introduced me to Jan, was discharged from the Navy and moved back to Findlay with his wife and their two young girls. He and his wife had been married in a UCC church in Findlay and then moved to California, where he was stationed. We resumed our close relationship with our friends, visiting back and forth. We went through a real emergency with them when their youngest child came down with a high fever that would not break. We sat up with them all night, taking turns bathing the child with cold water to help bring the fever down. When morning came, the fever had broken, and she recovered with almost no ill effects.

One evening we were visiting with our friends, and a couple of men from an independent Evangelical Church near where we lived stopped by to welcome us all to Findlay. The men were pleasant and welcoming to both families, so we began attending the church. Jan and I were both baptized as members of the church in 1966.

I was still struggling with my gender identity. I was suppressing my feelings and any expression of those feelings as much as possible. Jan wasn't discussing the issue with me, but she constantly feared that this would cause us to break up. We both had come from restrictive church experiences. I came from the Catholic Church, and Jan from a Pentecostal background. The simple message of the Evangelical Church convinced me that if I became as good a Christian as possible, my gender conflict would evaporate. I was an early believer in the conversion therapy practiced by so many Evangelical Christians today.

As I began to study the beliefs of the church, I had many conversations with the pastor there. As time went on, I realized that becoming as perfect a Christian as I could might involve becoming a Christian minister. I discussed it with our pastor, and he encouraged me. We took a trip to visit a Christian Bible seminary where our pastor had graduated. I discussed my thinking with the church board of elders. They also encouraged me and offered some support. We finally decided to move to Cincinnati so I could attend the seminary to study for the ministry.

During this time, I also took on a couple of extra part-time jobs. One job was at a local Marathon gas station, where I pumped gas and did general automotive maintenance. Jan also took on a part-time job working as a secretary/receptionist at the office of a local insurance representative. I took another part-time job as an announcer on a local radio station. The station had both AM and FM transmitters, and I had to keep both of them on the air in the evening until they signed off after midnight. The FM station was automated, so I just had to make sure that the right tapes were running; I also did the news broadcasts. On the AM side, I usually worked weekend mornings. Sunday mornings were interesting since I had to play several pre-taped religious programs, in addition to monitoring a couple of live broadcasts from local churches.

Those became important as I moved forward in my ministerial studies, since I listened to many different religious viewpoints. It also was a lesson to me that not all religious folk were very nice. It was my job to manage the start and end times of the programs, making sure that the schedule was maintained properly. I had one pastor who used a live hookup to his church and tended to stretch the limit of his end time. I spoke to management about the issue. They spoke to the pastor, telling him that I had been instructed to terminate the program on time, regardless of his situation. I began cutting him off mid-sentence in his sermon, which made him very angry. He came storming down to the station one Monday and complained loudly and heatedly about this, only to be told that the remedy for the problem was for him to end his sermons on time.

In July of 1968, Jan and I attended a church convention in Cincinnati, along with some friends from our church. During the convention, we took some time to tour Northern Kentucky with our friends, visiting some of the sites in the area that were important to the history of the church movement. As we traveled the area, we stopped at a roadside farm store and purchased some fresh tomatoes. Jan was six months pregnant, and she sat in the back seat devouring tomatoes as we toured.

I had been accepted as a student at the seminary, so we also took time to locate an apartment in the area where we could live. When we returned to Findlay after the convention, we began our move to Cincinnati. I borrowed Jan's stepfather's truck and made several trips back and forth down I-75 to Cincinnati to get us moved into our new apartment. By the end of July, we had completed the move, and we went looking for jobs there in Cincinnati. Our managers in the Ohio Bell telephone office in Findlay had assured us that our job experiences in their offices would allow us to transfer easily to the Cincinnati Bell office. When we got to Cincinnati, we discovered that we would be treated like any new person applying for a job. Since Cincinnati Bell was an independent company (not a part of the Bell System companies), our experience and positions in Ohio Bell meant nothing. Although the central office and operators' supervisors were anxious to utilize our experience, the HR department managers rejected our employment applications. We were both rejected following our medical exams because the examining doctors determined that we were both overweight and would be health risks as employees.

This experience was a real discouraging setback. We had set out on this path with the understanding that the Bell System would transfer our jobs with the telephone company. Now we had moved to a new city with no employment, and Jan was pregnant. I found employment with an insurance company that specialized in what was known as weekly premium insurance. Many low-income clients paid a few dollars each week for their life insurance. I was assigned to a Northern Kentucky area to visit clients each week and collect their weekly payments. It was a difficult job, but it was a good learning experience. My collection area in Northern Kentucky was in some of the lowest income areas of Covington and Newport.

One of the buildings in Newport that I had to collect from was a brothel, and the madam and a number of the girls were clients. At first, they offered to pay me in services. When they found out that I was married and a ministerial student, they were very understanding and were some of the best-paying clients. One of the things I learned from this experience was that insurance companies often try to avoid their responsibilities to pay for claims. One of the reasons I left the company was that I had several low-income customers who had experienced some medical issues. The company was delaying and refusing to pay claims. These issues had serious effects on the claimants' health and mental states. I tried to go to bat for them with the company, with little success, and was told basically to mind my own job and not worry about the claims department's job.

During this time frame, I searched for another job that was more related to my technical experience and was fortunate to find an opportunity to work with an electronics repair shop close by where we were living. My task was mainly to repair audio equipment for various high-end hi-fi sound systems that the repair shop had contracts to cover in- and out-of-warranty repairs. This job offered flexible hours, so I could go to class at the seminary in the morning and then work in the afternoon and evening. The job was challenging. The owners of the equipment that I was working on were often audiophiles who were very demanding and critical.

Often, we would get complaints that their equipment was not working properly, even though it was working within specifications, but not up to the owner's high standards. Also, the shop owner had contracted with some very low-end equipment manufacturers. These units were prone to defects, and, because of the nature of the manufacturing process, our only option was to replace the entire circuit board and associated wiring. The shop was also involved in designing and installing high-end sound systems in churches and auditoriums in the area. I learned the installation requirements of these facilities by assisting the shop owner as he bid on and installed the systems.

In the October of 1968, our son was born in Cincinnati at Christ Hospital. I had started my seminary studies in September, and the office at the seminary had recommended an obstetrician that several other married students had used. Jan began her labor at about 11:00 p.m., Sunday night, and our son was born at 3:00 p.m. on Monday. I was allowed to stay with Jan for a short time, but when she was taken into the labor room early in the morning, I was told to go to the fathers' room to wait for the birth. I sat there with the other fathers, all of us waiting to be called so that we could see our new child and spouse.

As the morning wore on, the fathers in the room with me were called out one by one until I was left alone by noontime. By about 1:00 p.m., I buzzed the intercom system and got no answer. I was somewhat concerned because I hadn't heard anything about Jan's condition since early morning. I walked down one hall and looked down another, at the nurses' station, and it was empty. There didn't appear to be anybody around to give me any information. So, I finally went back to the fathers' room and sat and waited. A little later on, I buzzed the intercom again and finally got a response. The nurse told me that Jan was still in labor; I would be notified when the child was born.

I was so glad when I was called eventually and told that our son was born and in perfect condition, and that Jan was just fine. It was one of the greatest days of my life. Jan and I took him home a couple of days later, and we began to share the responsibilities of parenthood. Jan would try to let me sleep through most of the nighttime feedings because she was sensitive to the fact that I was going to school and working and didn't have much time. I did, however, learn how to change diapers. At that time, we were using cloth diapers, and they were quite a process to maintain. But we got through that issue.

Eventually, Jan began working as a receptionist/secretary in the repair shop where I worked. She maintained the reports to the warranty companies and handled equipment intake and trouble write-ups. We hired some seminary students to care for our son when we were working away from the house. We settled in for several years of school, work, church, parenting, etc.

I took a weekend ministry at a church in Switzerland County in Southern Indiana during that time. I enjoyed preaching, and we loved the members of that small country church. Each Sunday afternoon, we would go to one of the members' homes for lunch and then return to the church for evening service. We fondly remembered our experiences with several elderly members who came to love us, and we cared for them deeply.

One of our memorable experiences there concerned the outhouse the church utilized. Like many churches, they often had "revival" services, usually a week-long time for meetings. During the services, a well-known preacher would come and deliver nightly messages designed to encourage the growth of the membership. This particular revival was being conducted at our church. Jan, our son, and I were hosting the speaker at the church. One afternoon, one of us had to use the outhouse and noticed that someone had written the date the church dedicated the outhouse on the wall. It happened to be that day which was the anniversary of the dedication date. So, we took it upon ourselves to go out the back of the church building, to the outhouse, and stand there around the outhouse and sing "Happy Birthday" to it.

We always remembered our time at that church and even took a trip back there many years later when we lived in Louisville, Kentucky. The church had been closed, sold, and subsequently remodeled into a private home by the time we visited.

Mid-November 1971 was one of the most difficult periods of our lives. We were still living in Cincinnati, and our son was three years old. We were expecting another child to come into our family, and Jan struggled through her pregnancy. The baby was particularly active and making Jan most uncomfortable. She felt the beginning of labor pains on Saturday night and called her obstetrician. She found out then that he was out of town for the weekend and that his practice partner, whom Jan had never met, was covering for him. Jan was told to go to the hospital and, once there, was sent to a labor room.

I was with her through the night as her labor pains came and went. In the early morning, the nurses left us alone for several hours, and it seemed as if her labor pains abated. Finally, I went and located a nurse to check Jan. She checked her and went to call the doctor at home. He came in, and he and the nurse checked Jan again. Fetal monitors had not become available at that time, but the doctor was very concerned and told us that Jan needed to go to surgery for an immediate C-section. We asked them to leave the labor room for a couple of minutes. We prayed and then called them back in to prepare for the surgery.

Jan was taken to surgery, and I was sent to a waiting room. Sometime later, they called me to meet the doctor. He told me that our baby boy was stillborn. The cord was knotted and wrapped around his neck, and he suffocated. We were devastated. When I was allowed to visit Jan, she was inconsolable. She believed she had felt the baby move only hours before the birth. We decided to name him Mark. We stayed together for a few hours, and then I went to call family, friends, and our church family to let them know what happened. Later I went home and stopped with our upstairs neighbors to pick up our son, who was staying with them while Jan and I were at the hospital. As I carried him downstairs to our apartment, I was overcome with grief and sat down on the landing of the steps and just held him and cried, rocking back and forth on the landing. I don't think he ever understood just how much he meant to me at that moment. His presence gave me some hope for the future, and I prayed we could carry on with our lives despite this tragedy.

Mark was cremated. We were given no option to have a funeral; we were not given his ashes or death certificate. We were just expected to pick up our lives and carry on as if nothing happened. But this affected our lives in ways no one knew. Jan, from that time on, was reluctant to think about having other children. The trauma of carrying a child to full-term, only to have it die in the birth process, was too much for her to contemplate.

I knew that Jan always remembered that date as his birthday. She rarely spoke of him, even to me, but she contacted the hospital and the Cincinnati records bureau a few years ago, and they sent her a copy of his death certificate. One of the things Jan and I talked about in her last days was that Mark would be waiting to welcome her. She was comforted by that thought.

In 1972 Jan got an opportunity to work as an insurance agent for a major insurance company in downtown Cincinnati. She received her insurance agent's license and was an agent for auto and homeowner's insurance policies, managing over 1,200 client accounts. Around that time, we started sending our son to nursery preschool. Each morning as we put him in the school's station wagon, he screamed. The driver told us that he screamed all the way down the street until he was out of our sight. Then he quieted down and enjoyed learning and playing at the day nursery. It was a great place, and they gave him a good foundation for starting school.

I graduated from seminary in 1973 with a degree in ministry. The following semester I began graduate studies in theology. During this time, I continued working at the repair shop. I also began working with the seminary to rebuild their recording studios and took charge of an illegal, student-run radio station. Previously, someone had set up a legal carrier current campus radio station. The FCC permits this type of station to operate unlicensed. According to the FCC, "a carrier current station consists of an AM radio frequency signal on a frequency between 535 and 1705 kHz injected into a power line. The effective service range of a carrier current station is approximately 200 feet (61 meters) from the power line; however, a carrier current signal will not pass through a utility transformer."[13]

Some students had taken it upon themselves to disconnect the transmitter from the power lines and connect it to an antenna that could radiate the signal. The object of this exercise was to allow the girls' dorm, which was on a separate power transformer, to get coverage for the signal so that the station deejays could have their girlfriends listen to their programs. Unfortunately, since the seminary is situated on a hill overlooking downtown Cincinnati, the installed antenna allowed the broadcast signal to be heard clearly several miles away into the downtown area. This operation was a serious violation of FCC rules and put the seminary in jeopardy of paying a hefty fine.

There was no faculty supervision of the facility during this period, and when I heard what was going on, I was appalled. By that time, I had my first-class FCC general (commercial) radio license and my advanced class amateur (ham radio) FCC license. I understood exactly what the violations entailed. I disabled the external antenna and reconnected the transmitter to the power line to operate legally, and went to the school administration and informed them of the situation. I was put in charge of the recording facilities and the radio station.

---

[13] "https://www.fcc.gov/media/radio/low-power-radio-general-information

The facility was in poor condition. No wiring diagrams were available to show how the equipment was interconnected, and much of the equipment was not functional. With the help of my then six-year-old son I took on the task of rewiring the studio and recording the various connections. The school also decided to apply for an FM station license to make everything legal. I contacted an engineer who could guide us through the application process. Eventually, we had to drop the effort because the only available frequency was also being applied for by an area university that was much larger. The seminary administration did not want to go through the effort and expense of a battle with a state-funded institution.

I continued to work at the stereo repair shop and part-time at a religious radio station in Northern Kentucky as an announcer and engineer. In 1974 I was invited to become a staff member at the seminary. I managed the recording studio and the carrier current radio station and developed a ham radio station capable of communicating with missionaries around the world. In addition, I was assigned to teach freshman English and religious broadcasting courses.

With Jan working at the insurance company and my being staff at the seminary, our salaries would be a little more stable. We decided to move from our apartment in the Western Hills section of Cincinnati and buy a house. We found a small two-bedroom house in the Westwood area of Cincinnati and moved in the summer of 1974. Also, in the fall of 1974, our son began grade school. He was still five years old when he started first grade; his sixth birthday was not until October. Because of that, he was required to be tested. That was done at Central Fairmount Public School, close to our new house, to see if he was ready to start the first grade. When the evaluator determined that he was ready for first grade, we decided to enroll him in Central Fairmount School, but, before the school year started, I talked with another staff member at the seminary who lived in our area. He told me he was sending his son to an area Lutheran school. We looked into it and decided to enroll our son there instead. He began first grade in September 1974 and had a marvelous first-grade teacher. When the teacher tried to get our son to read, he refused. He said that he didn't need to read since we would read to him whatever he needed. She finally convinced him that he wanted to learn to read for himself, and so began a lifetime of reading.

From the fall of 1974 to the spring of 1977, I worked for the seminary, teaching and developing the radio ministry there. I had several students who were interested in radio ministries and music recording. One of them was a young man who was an amazing piano player, singer, and songwriter. He was very popular among the student body and often gave impromptu concerts, singing many of his own compositions. We recorded a demo tape in the seminary chapel, and I took it to Nashville, where a former CBS student who had become a popular Christian music artist lived. We never heard back from anyone in Nashville; however, the young man became a popular Christian musician and hymn writer. One of his compositions became very popular and has been included in many Christian hymnals. I lost touch with him after I left the seminary, but found out later that he had died tragically in 1997 in an automobile accident.

In 1977 the seminary had some financial issues, and they decided to cut back on staff. As one of the staff members with the least seniority, I was told that I would be let go. I decided to apply to the University of Cincinnati (UC) Broadcasting Department for graduate studies. In the fall of 1977, I was accepted and given a graduate assistant position at UC. As a graduate assistant, I was assigned to teach broadcast equipment operation and audio production courses. These were required courses for students in the undergrad broadcasting program.

One of the interesting benefits of my graduate assistant position was that the other grad assistant, with whom I shared an office, was a native of Maine. He had grown up in South Portland and was doing grad work in the broadcast law field. We had lots of discussions about growing up in New England. In the process, he mentioned that he had a cabin on Sebago Lake in Southwestern Maine. It was an inheritance from his grandfather, who had built the cabin. He offered to let us use the cabin anytime we wanted. That began our annual vacation trips to New England. The cabin's septic system was not very good, so the water to the bathroom toilet had been disconnected. To flush the toilet, we had to get a bucket of water from the lake to pour into the toilet's tank. This requirement precipitated a lot of trips to the lake to fetch buckets of water. We made this task our son's job, and nicknamed him Running Water.

Each summer, we would vacation for two weeks at the cabin. We drove to Boston and visited my parents in Waltham on the way up to Maine. We stayed in the cabin for two weeks, with a day trip back to Boston for sightseeing and another stop in Waltham, then returned to Cincinnati with another stop on the way through Waltham to check on my parents. Each year, as we visited them, it became obvious that my parents were declining in health. Finally, we decided to move back to the Boston area. Despite past conflicts, as their only child, I felt responsible for taking care of them.

At the time we decided to move back to Boston, I was teaching vocational electronics at a Cincinnati high school, and Jan was working at an area publishing company. In 1978

I completed my graduate studies at UC (except for the master's thesis, which never did get done). I had begun working at a local TV station as a "vacation relief engineer," filling in for full-time staff engineers who were on vacation. Since it was not a full-year employment situation, I looked for a more permanent position and found one teaching in the Cincinnati public school system beginning in the fall of 1978. It was almost ideal since the summer vacation from teaching allowed me to continue my summertime job with the TV station.

The problem was that when I was working both jobs, there was an overlap for a month or so in both spring and fall. I taught school during the day, left there at 3:00 p.m. or so, and went to the TV station, where I usually worked a 4:00 p.m. to 12:00 a.m., or 6:00 p.m. to 2:00 a.m., shift. Spending time with Jan and our son was impossible. I was getting worn out fast, and my relationship with Jan was deteriorating. I survived the summers of 1978 and 1979 working that way, until the TV station decided that they needed me to extend my time with them, starting in March and ending in December. That was more of an overlap than I could handle, so I resigned from there in the fall of 1979.

I was able to find another part-time job teaching broadcast engineering at a local technical college. The course was designed to help students pass the test for a first-class FCC commercial license. I also continued to teach the audio production course as an adjunct instructor at UC.

From 1977 to 1979, Jan worked as church secretary for a local church. Then, early in 1979, she started working at a publishing company as a department secretary for the Special Products department. Jan's work involved proofreading books and special publications. This work included games and puzzle books. One of Jan's favorite projects was proofreading "hidden word" puzzle books. Many of them were designed for teens and young adults. Jan's task was to make sure there were no "bad" words that the youth would find. She felt her experience as a sailor's wife had given her a distinct edge in locating the "bad" words.

On May 25, 1979, Jan was at work when she got a phone call from her boss, who was traveling to a booksellers' convention in Los Angeles and was on a stopover at Chicago O'Hare Airport. She had called in to talk to her husband, who also worked at the publishing company, and then she asked to be transferred to Jan in order to pass along some instructions regarding work issues. She talked to Jan for a few minutes and then hung up and got on her plane to LA— American Airlines Flight 191. The plane crashed on takeoff from O'Hare Airport, just after 3:00 p.m., when the left engine detached from the wing. All 260 passengers and crew died in the crash. I was working at the TV station, and I heard a news report of the crash and called Jan at work to see what flight her boss was on. I then called down to the newsroom to see if they had any information about the flight number and was told that it was 191. I called Jan back and confirmed that it was her boss's plane that had crashed. We were told at the time there were no survivors. Jan was heartbroken, but she had to go to her boss's husband and let him know about the crash. One of their teenage children also called Jan to find out the flight number, and Jan had to confirm that her mother was on the plane that crashed. Jan had made her boss's travel arrangements and was the last person to talk to her before she boarded the plane, so the episode profoundly affected Jan. Each year on May 25, she remembered her.

We were just trying to live our lives as a couple and raise our son during this time. We were like so many couples. The issues of our lives were money and time, in addition to my gender conflicts. We devoted our lives to making sure our son got whatever he needed to grow and prosper. He was a great son. He enjoyed school, learning, and reading.

In 1975 Jan asked me what I wanted for my birthday. I read about a new World Hockey Association (WHA) franchise in Cincinnati, the Stingers. Growing up in the Boston area, I was a Bruins fan, and I had skated on area ponds each winter. So, I requested tickets to a Stingers game for my birthday. That game triggered a love for hockey in our son. We had new additions to our busy schedules—hockey practices, games, hockey schools, and board meetings for the local Youth Hockey Association. We became even more involved in youth hockey when our son was chosen for a travel team. The team went all over the Midwestern area, from Fort Wayne, Indiana, to Cleveland, Ohio, and various destinations in between.

Hockey was the cause of the only time that I can remember striking our son. One of the boys in our son's class in school was also on two of his hockey teams, the house team and the travel team. The two boys were intensely competitive. Our son was one of the top students in the class, always getting As. The other boy was not a good student, consistently getting low marks. However, our son was a slower skater and infrequently scored goals on the hockey teams, while the other boy was a fast skater and a good shot, scoring the most goals on the team. This disparity in the two environments produced some jealous competition, and out of it came an incident that really shook our family.

We believe that our son's classmate started a rumor on the travel team that our son was cursing and fighting with the players on the team. The story grew—we believe encouraged by our son's classmate—and finally came to the attention of many of the other players' parents. They came as a group to us and demanded that we control our son.

We couldn't believe this story because it was so contrary to all we knew about our son. But it was hard to discount the rumor when it seemed to be coming from all the rest of the team and numerous parents. Our son was a quiet boy who was mostly interested in schoolwork. He enjoyed playing hockey, but it wasn't going to be his life's work. Many of the other parents on the travel team encouraged their sons to improve their abilities and compete for college hockey scholarships. Our son, Jan, and I thought this was just a fun activity, but we encouraged him to become as good as possible. We sent him to skating classes and hockey schools to improve his ability, but we had no notion that he would be good enough to get a college scholarship.

The accusation from the other parents came as a complete shock to us. We couldn't believe a group of parents had come to us and demanded that we punish our son; we just didn't understand it. We went to our son, but he denied the accusations and told us that it was a story made up by his classmate. We couldn't understand how one boy could influence the whole team and make them repeat this story to their parents. The parents insisted that we control our son, so as our son was going to bed, I went into his room to question him further. I demanded that he tell the truth. He insisted that he had. I told him that if he didn't tell the truth, I would have to punish him. He repeated that he was telling the truth. I struck him twice, but he tearfully protested his innocence. There is that old saying about "it'll hurt me more than you," and it certainly did in this case.

I've always regretted that incident. We never really got an explanation from anyone, and we never found out what actually happened, but that incident damaged my relationship with my son.

As we became active in the local Youth Hockey association, we became friends with some of the Stingers players. One was a New England native, so he and I had several conversations about New England and shared our love for coffee ice cream. Jan became friends with the Stingers goalie, and our son followed another Stinger player. When the WHA folded and merged with the NHL in 1979, the Quebec Nordiques picked up all three of our favorites. To visit our new friends, in 1980 we drove to St. Louis and Chicago when the Nordiques had games in those cities. We stayed in the same hotels the players stayed in, had breakfast with them, and visited after the games.

Where was my gender conflict during those years? We were so busy that it was difficult for me to find time to cross-dress, as much as I needed it to find some release from the gender conflict. I went months without any opportunity. Jan had the idea I was cross-dressing all the time. We had some discussions about the issue, and as I became more depressed, I decided that I needed some counseling.

One of the members of our church was a counselor, and he and his female counseling partner agreed to help us. We had joint sessions and sessions in which I met alone with the male counselor while Jan met with the lady counselor. One day he told me that I could not continue to go through the bouts of depression. He said that I needed to deal with the issue or it would destroy me. He also sent me to a psychiatrist who diagnosed me as a transvestite. At that time, the term *transgender* was not yet in widespread use. I continued to struggle with the issue, and Jan and I rarely discussed it. It was not until we moved to New England that we began dealing with my gender identity.

In 1982 our son was in the eighth grade at a college-prep high school rooted in a classical liberal arts curriculum for grades seven through twelve. I was teaching electronics in a Cincinnati high school, and Jan was working at the publishing company. That summer, we went on our annual trip to Sebago Lake, Maine, and visited my parents.

It was clear to us that my parents needed help. My father had fallen down our basement steps and suffered damage to his esophagus that prevented his eating solid food. He was living on liquid protein drinks. Ironically, Jan later suffered from a similar problem when radiation treatments for her breast cancer damaged the muscle that controls the passage of food from the esophagus to the stomach.

At the time of our visit, Jan and I noticed that my father, who was always a very thin person, had lost weight and was having difficulty getting around. My mother, who had experienced several attacks that today would be called TIAs, was on a pacemaker, and her ability to get around was limited. Since my father had been my mother's caregiver for many years, I questioned him about his condition, and during the discussion, I asked him for the name of his doctor.

When we returned to Cincinnati, I called his doctor and asked how my father was doing. My father found out and responded by changing doctors so that I could not track his condition. At that point, we decided that we probably should move back to Massachusetts to monitor my parents' health more closely.

I began researching possible teaching jobs in Massachusetts. I found out that I had to pass a state exam in order to be a certified vocational teacher. It was a two-part process; the first was a written test, and the second was a practical lab test. I scheduled the first test.

Jan told the story of our move in our 1983 Christmas letter:

> *Ted flew to Boston in March to take a written test for his Mass. teacher's certificate. When he returned to Boston at the end of April to take the "practical" part of the test, the whole family went along to visit his parents. At that time, we knew that his father was declining rapidly.*
>
> *On May 23, Ted's father passed away, and his mom went to a nursing home—one where she had done a lot of volunteer work years ago. After school let out, Ted and our son returned to Boston, staying in his parents' home in Waltham, to help his mom settle in the nursing home and look for a job for Ted. Ted, his mom, and our son had two good weeks together. She seemed to be recovering from the loss of her husband and seemed to be comfortable in the nursing home. Ted found a job teaching electronics at a high school north of Boston, so they returned to Cincinnati on the weekend of the Fourth of July.*
>
> *We all returned to Boston a week later so that I could look for a job. When we visited Ted's mom, we found that she had taken a turn for the worse. The doctor seemed to feel that she had suffered a slight stroke. After finding a job with an electronics company in Burlington, MA, northwest of Boston, we returned to Cincinnati to get packed for the move. While we were back in Ohio, the doctor called to tell us that Ted's mom had suffered another stroke but had stabilized.*
>
> *We left Cincinnati on August 19 and arrived at 5:30 a.m. on Sunday, August 21. I began my new job the next day, while Ted and our son finished unloading the moving*

van, storing most of our furniture in a garage at our church, and taking the essentials to his parents' home in Waltham.

We discovered that Ted's mom had suffered a massive stroke, which left her completely paralyzed. After a short hospital stay, she returned to the nursing home, where she continued to decline. She could not move or communicate, so her death on October 5 was a blessing to her, bringing her peace and reuniting her with her husband.

We decided that we would move to Wilmington, MA, because of the location and the high school there offered the type and quality of courses that we wanted our son to have. Our son started his sophomore year in high school, and Ted started teaching in September.

Jan left a few things out of her letter. First, when my father's doctor called to tell me of his passing, the first question he asked was if I was Richard's son. After the doctor told me of my father's death, he told me that my father had told him he had no children. After his death, the doctor asked my mother if there was anyone else he should notify, and my mother told him he should notify me since I was their son. He was shocked to hear that my father had a son. It was an indication of just how upset my father was with my abandonment of their church. He had also specifically written in his will that Jan, our son, and I should receive just a few dollars from his estate. Following my father's death, his lawyer worked with my mother to change the conditions of her will to name me as her sole heir, removing the restrictions my father had included in his.

Another thing that occurred when our son and I returned to Waltham so that I could look for a job. One day I was going through my father's desk, where he kept his important papers. I found a letter to my father from the lawyer who handled my adoption. He summarized my history, listing my birth mother's name and indicating where she was living at that time. He also indicated that I was adopted twice and that my first adoptive mother had passed away in April of 1947. My adoption was made official on March 11, 1949.

Up until the moment I read that letter, I thought that I was adopted only once and that my birth mother was the person who had died when I was young. I sat in the chair at my father's desk for some time, reading that letter over and over, absorbing the implication that my birth mother could be alive. There was too much happening at the time for me to take any action on the information. I did tell Jan and our son what I had found. It was sometime later when I decided to search for my birth mother and made contact with her.

Also, when our son and I stayed in Waltham, we had several visits with my mother in the nursing home and were able a couple of times to take her out to dinner at one of my parents' favorite restaurants. Those visits gave me a chance to resolve the conflicts I had with my mother. When I questioned her about some of the incidents of abuse that I remembered, she clearly had no memory of them. At that point, she just seemed to be happy having me there, and seeing our son gave her great pleasure. I was able to put to rest the ill feelings that I harbored for her.

The trip from Cincinnati in August was a difficult one. We stopped in Ohio to pick up our friend Ron, and he drove the moving truck from there to Massachusetts. Jan, our son, and I rode in our car, along with our cat, Tigger. Unfortunately, it was very hot, and the air conditioning in our car was not working very well. Tigger did not travel well and ended up with heat stroke. He lived through the trip, but he died shortly after we arrived in Massachusetts. A few weeks later, we drove into Boston to Angell Memorial Animal Adoption Center and adopted two kittens—brothers—whom we named Patches and Mittens. Since then, we have always had at least two cats—always rescues—in our house.

We arrived in Waltham and stored most of our furniture from Cincinnati in the basement of my parents' house, and we stored the rest in a building on our church's property. Jan started work, and our son and I began organizing the house in Waltham. We had decided where we would live, so we received permission for our son to start his sophomore year at the high school in that community. We were working with a real estate agent to find a place to live there. I started teaching junior class students at a North Shore high school in the electronics program.

My mother passed away in early October. We found our new home, sold the house in Waltham, moved in during Christmas break, and settled into our new life in Massachusetts.

Jan mentioned in her story that, through a call to a help line, I had been referred to Tiffany Club in Wayland. It took me some time to get up the courage to call them and another long time to decide to meet with them. The directions to the club were somewhat involved. I was to drive out Route 20 (Boston Post Road) to the center of Wayland and locate the town library. I was to park in the library lot and go over to a phone booth in the corner of the lot and call the club phone number I had been given. I followed those instructions and was interviewed on the phone for several minutes, and then they decided they would come down and meet me there in the parking lot to continue the interview.

It took a half hour or so before a couple of the club members drove into the parking lot and came over to my car. There were a few questions, and then they invited me to come to sit in their car. They were the first people I had seen cross-dressed. They were dressed very fashionably. They interviewed me for about half an hour or forty-five minutes, asking several questions about my experiences with cross-dressing. I told them about my history and that I had been diagnosed by a psychiatrist in Cincinnati as a transvestite. They agreed that I could go to the clubhouse to continue the interview process and learn more about membership.

I followed them in my car to a house on a side road, back close to the Sudbury River. I parked in a cul-de-sac and walked to the house, which was set back off the road and under some trees. When I entered, I saw some cross-dressed people sitting around and chatting. In the living room more people were sitting, watching TV, and talking. I then went to the house's basement, where clothes were hanging. Also down there were changing rooms and, along the wall, a long table with a mirror, which were suitable for putting on makeup, fixing hair, and so forth. I noticed that there were some females. A few were cross-dressed as males, but most appeared to be wives of the club members.

I went home and told Jan about my visit. We discussed the initiation fee and annual costs involved in membership of the club and decided that Tiffany Club might be a good place to get some answers and help us understand more about why I had these feelings. For several months I visited the club by myself on the regular night that was open for members. I took some clothes and makeup with me to become more familiar with the process. I also chatted with some of the members and their wives. Several of the wives asked me to invite Jan.

She was very reluctant but decided that she needed to learn more about that part of my life. She came out with me and eventually became active in the wives' support group there. I also became more active and was elected to the board of directors.

I was introduced to the owner of the house, Merissa Sherrill Lynn. I found out later that Merissa was the person who answered my first call to the club. Merissa had founded the Tiffany Club in her home in Wayland after she had been involved with the transgender community for many years. She established the club as a support group for all facets of the "trans" community. After initially purchasing the house in Wayland with help from others, she eventually was able to pay it off with money from an inheritance. She had several tenants in the building, but she kept a bedroom and workroom for herself in the basement. The main areas of the house—the living room, kitchen, and majority of the basement—were public areas available to members of the club.

Merissa was a special person. She was a former ski instructor with a BA in philosophy and an ex-army ranger. She had struggled to find her place in society, like so many of us. Once she finally began to accept herself, Merissa started trying to find others who, like her, were transsexual. She found that most of the support was for male cross-dressers. She became a member of a Boston group called Cherrystone and was active in setting up regional gatherings like Ariadne Kane's Fantasia Fair, held annually in Provincetown. Focused on helping others, Merissa founded Tiffany Club in 1978. She understood the value of having a permanent location for members to assemble, so she began to search for a home. First, she rented a home in Weston, and then she found a permanent spot in Wayland that she purchased. There, she invited all facets of the gender spectrum to come and participate in discussions and be accepted for who they were. Unfortunately, the interactions were not always friendly, and there were some bitter disagreements from time to time.

Jan and I grew to love Merissa and appreciate her sometimes abrasive personality. While Jan became active in the wives' support group, I began to assist Merissa in editing the *Tapestry*, the Tiffany Club newsletter and a magazine for the wider trans community. One of the issues that Jan and I both had with the wives' support group was the constant negativity expressed by the wives. Merissa mentions an experience she and a friend of hers had while visiting another wives' group in the early '70s:

> *She told me being with these women was like swimming in vitriol. She had nothing to say. They were bitter, and she wasn't bitter. They were angry, and she wasn't angry. They weren't even remotely supportive of their partners; she was very supportive. She had nothing to say. I had nothing to say. What a strange experience. However, it taught me several things, such as how deeply set fear and ignorance was, how desperately wives needed an adequate support system, and finding other people like myself was not easy.*[14]

Jan was able to get along with the other ladies in the wives' group at Tiffany, even though she was growing more supportive of me and many of the other wives were openly critical and sometimes hateful toward their spouses.

One of the first tasks Merissa gave me was reviewing articles submitted for publication. I found that most of the articles were stories of "My First Time Out in Public Cross-

---

[14] MSL-Kerri. Merissa Sherrill Lynn, Her History as She Wrote It, Kindle edition. Pp 103, 104

dressed." I quickly found that these stories were all similar, and it was difficult to determine which ones to accept and which ones to reject. Jan was helpful since she had a lifetime of experience as a proofreader and editor. We assisted Merissa with the preparation of several issues of *Tapestry* and tried to help her become more current with the publication of the magazine. Since the magazine had become more than just a Tiffany newsletter and was a national publication with a large, paying subscription base, she had an obligation to publish on a regular schedule. However, Merissa had not made that a priority and was quite lax about it.

Merissa began getting more opportunities to expand her influence nationally and internationally. Her Tiffany responsibilities were preventing her from doing many of the things that she wished to do. This recognition led to her founding the International Foundation for Gender Education (IFGE). She decided that IFGE needed to be a nonprofit, so she transferred the IRS nonprofit 501(C)(3) status from Tiffany Club to the new organization, IFGE, in 1986. This move created a problem with the Tiffany Club; it lost its nonprofit status. If IFGE was to be a national organization, then, as a local organization, Tiffany Club needed to be separate from IFGE. After a major disagreement with the Tiffany Club board of directors, Merissa and Tiffany Club parted ways; IFGE found offices in Waltham, and Tiffany Club of New England (TCNE) was born.

Jan and I continued to work with Merissa, editing *Tapestry* and working on projects for IFGE. In 1991 Jan and I co-edited a book for IFGE, *Wives, Partners, and Others*, which was a compilation of several articles published in various issues of *Tapestry* over the years. The articles were all from and for those who were living with a cross-dresser.

The Tiffany board decided that the club needed its own newsletter, and Jan and I were "volunteered" to publish it. After much discussion, the name *RoseBuds*, as suggested by Jan, was picked for the newsletter, and with Merissa's permission, we adopted the rose-and-hands logo used for *Tapestry*. January of 1987 brought the publication of the first issue of *RoseBuds*. Jan and I continued to assist Merissa with *Tapestry* when we could. We worked with the Tiffany board and published the newsletter for some time.

Unfortunately, this activity created a problem with our son since we initially had to hide the nature of the group with whom we were meeting. In addition, we had counseling sessions and other meetings and were trying to maintain a normal connection to our church. Finally, after our break with the church, we talked with our son and told him everything.

Why Did I Delay Transition?

Today, there is much more known about gender identity issues than was available when I was a young child. It is common for children of a young age to begin transitioning to the gender with which they feel most comfortable. Parents are becoming more aware of the consequences of forcing their children to live with the gender conflict. When I was growing up, I had no idea why I had the feelings I did. I had no idea it was possible to change genders until the news about Christine Jorgensen's transition was made public. Even then, the resulting coverage made it clear that this was not an option for me. During my teenage years, I thought that, once I found a girl to marry, the problem would be solved, and it would all go away. When I met and married Jan, I discovered that wasn't the solution either.

I also tried religion. I thought that if I became a perfect Christian, that would make it go away. Not!! Despite what many Evangelical Christians believe, you can't make it go away by being a faithful Christian. I discovered that forcing myself to avoid acting on my feelings worked for a while, but instead of making it go away, exactly the opposite occurred. The longer I tried to control the impulses I felt, the stronger they became and the tenser I became. It was a constant spiral into depression. If I acted on the impulse and cross-dressed,

I felt weak and more depressed. I went through cycles of depression that drove me further into the depths.

When Jan and I began to learn more about the issue of gender identity through our involvement with Tiffany and IFGE, we started to understand that this was not going to go away. In the controlled environment of Tiffany and the various events they held, I was able to find some relief from the conflicts I was feeling by experiencing times when I could become the woman I felt I should be. Unfortunately, we both began to realize that the temporary relief I got from a weekend away in Provincetown or another event had a downside. The emotional "high" I felt when I was experiencing one of those events mirrored the extreme "low" I felt when the event was over. The solution was temporary, and I began to understand that my only solution was a permanent transition.

I came to that conclusion in the early 1990s. We began to back out of membership in Tiffany and IFGE, and we began meeting with a counselor experienced in dealing with gender identity issues. The counselor helped me to work through my fear of transition. We participated in support groups, moderated by our counselor, designed to assist couples and wives of trans persons. My major fear of transition was losing Jan and my relationship with our son.

One of the main reasons I delayed my transition was my obligation to Jan and our son. I did not want to disrupt our son's development and put him through the turmoil I was experiencing. We had told him about my gender identity issues when we left our church, but, after, he wanted very little conversation about the subject. It was clear he had put up some barriers.

After he completed graduate school in 1997 and his marriage in 1999, we determined that he was appropriately embarking on establishing his life as a mature thirty-plus-year-old adult. He was establishing his life separate from us as his parents, and rightly so. Jan and I had several discussions about our feelings of loss. We felt that my gender issues contributed to his desire to distance himself from us socially.

Jan and I also discussed plans for our future together as we approached retirement. A large part of that centered on where I was going with my gender identity. Part of the reason I had begun, in the early '90s, to distance us from our activities with Tiffany Club and gender counselors was the dawning realization that I was transsexual. I realized that occasional cross-dressing was not a solution for me. One indication of this was the intense depression I felt each time I tried to return to "normal" life. Each time I left behind my cross-dressing experience, I experienced a deep depression for several days and a longing for the next opportunity I would have. Jan was well aware of these episodes, and we discussed on several occasions how we could resolve those feelings.

I became more aware that the solution was not one I wanted to think about—living full-time as a female. I had seen many friends and other members of Tiffany who had been through gender transition and watched as they felt the pain of loss of access to parents, wives, children, and other friends who could not accept their change of gender. I was petrified most of all that I would lose Jan. I had watched many married Tiffany members lose their spouses during the transition period.

As leaders of Tiffany, Jan and I had discussed with several of these couples some options that would allow them to remain together. We watched as many of them decided that they just would not be able to remain together. Many of the wives felt that they could not remain in a relationship with the woman that their husbands would become. On the other hand, the husband who was planning to transition was often unwilling to restrict their activities or the changes they planned to make in their lives. Many wives had problems with the makeup and extravagant dress habits their spouses were demanding. In addition, the planned surgery the trans person anticipated was difficult for wives to accept.

Witnessing others who shared our experiences helped us as we discussed our future. As I began to consider my options, it was clear that I could not continue to experience the periods of deep depression. I became more aware that my options were leading me in two different directions—transition or suicide. I had tried for over fifty-five years to exist with my gender conflict, and I could not see continuing to experience that ongoing turmoil in the future. As I approached my sixtieth birthday, I realized that the inner conflict must end, one way or the other. As I considered options, I realized that Jan had become comfortable with, and accepting of, my cross-dressing. Jan would have been happy if I limited my activities to that, but I knew that I would not be happy. So, that was not a solution for me.

As we approached the end of the century, Jan and I began to discuss our options. Like many trans persons, I had been thinking about these issues for some time. What cisgender persons don't understand is that a conflict of gender never leaves one's mind. For cisgender persons, there is no conflict. From the time I was a small child, the conflict never really left me. I remember Jan asked me once if I was happy. I told her that I was not and that I could never remember being happy. She asked me what would make me happy. I could not give her an answer because, at that time, I had no understanding of the source of the conflicting feelings I was experiencing.

I realized that the key to my successful transition would be a continuing relationship with Jan. I asked her, if I transitioned to live as a woman, would she remain with me. She thought for a minute and responded, "As of today, yes." She went on to tell me, "It's too late for me to train another partner!" Her response, "as of today," told me that our relationship depended on my ability to confine my changes to things that Jan could live with and accept. It would rely on my understanding of Jan and what she could accept. It meant that she would need to understand each change I was thinking of making, how it would occur, and why the change was needed.

For example, Jan had noted earlier, "One of the most difficult and emotional changes for me was when she had her ears pierced. I had become somewhat used to her dressing as a female, but getting her ears pierced was the one thing I had left that was mine alone. I felt sure then that I had lost my husband. It was really difficult emotionally." As I went through the transition process, I discussed with Jan when and how I would get my ears pierced. It was several months after I transitioned before I did it, and several more before I began to wear any earrings that were dressier than plain studs. Jan signaled her acceptance of this issue by purchasing some earrings for me as a gift.

There were at least two elements to Jan's acceptance. The first was agreeing to discuss changes well before they were implemented. The second was her understanding of the alternative. She had been with me at that point for over thirty-five years, and she had observed firsthand the effects my gender conflict. We had many discussions through the years, some lasting through the night. We had sleepless nights. We had arguments that ended with one or the other of us leaving the house and walking around the block or going for a drive. She was well aware that the alternative meant that she would be a widow. We had seen too many in the transgender community who had made that life-ending decision. In my case, she knew that I was a confirmed coward, which made it difficult to take that option. However, she also knew that I was getting to the end of my ability to manage the conflict, and, rather than risk my continuing turmoil or my permanently ending it, she decided that the best option for both of us was for me to transition.

I decided that I would do everything I could to mitigate the effects of my transition on Jan. I took everything as slowly as I could. Also, we began regular counseling with a gender specialist who had experience guiding couples through the transition process. Our counselor also had separate groups for wives of trans persons and a group for couples going through the transition. These two groups gave us connections that provided Jan significant support.

One of the groups that our counselor hosted was for couples dealing with the transition of one of the partners. One of the couples we met, Anne and Nancy, would become lifelong friends. Nancy and Jan shared the difficulty of being the spouse of a transsexual, with all the life turmoil that involved. Nancy became a real resource for Jan as we went through the changes that came with my transition.

During this period, I worked for a telecom company doing computer application development in Marlborough, Massachusetts. In 1999 I moved to a larger telecom company as a development manager in charge of a team of application developers around the country and Canada.

In 2000 we decided that I would begin my transition, and I began taking estrogen injections under the guidance of an endocrinologist. I began to experience physical and emotional changes. Late in 2000, I went to my manager and told him that I had begun the gender transition process. We began discussions with the HR department about how and when we would inform my team and other employees and customers about the transition.

In early 2001 several companies in the telecom industry suffered financial setbacks, and, in response, they began cutbacks. The company I was working for initiated a large layoff of employees, and I had to lay off several developers on my team. After that first round of layoffs, the company initiated a second round of layoffs that involved the development teams' consolidation. The process eliminated my team, and as the development manager with the least seniority, I was laid off in April 2001. I have been asked if my impending gender transition impacted the decision to lay me off, and I do not think it did. My manager and other higher-level company officials had given their unqualified support. In addition, the fact that I was not laid off in the first round indicates my transition was not the issue.

Jan and I had to make a difficult decision. Would I complete my transition and then begin job hunting as a female? Or, should I look for a new job and transition as an employee of the new company? I felt it would be better for any future employer to hire me after transition than to hire me as a male and then go through the turmoil of my transition after hiring me.

So, we decided that I would complete the transition process while unemployed. The first step was legally changing my name from Edward to Diane and getting a new driver's license with my corrected name and gender. At that point, Massachusetts did not have any specific Department of Motor Vehicles (DMV) regulations about a change of gender marker on licenses, so when an accepting DMV clerk went ahead and changed my gender marker to *F*, I was pleased.

In July 2001, I officially transitioned legally from male to female. Some elements of the transition would have to wait for later. I had not completed any surgery that would allow a change of birth certificate, which, at that time, was allowed in Massachusetts only with a surgery letter.

With my legal transition completed, I began to look for another position that would utilize my years of experience as a programmer and manager of computer programmers. I edited my resume and notified my previous employers that they might be getting inquiries for employment history for me using my transition name and gender. As I searched for a new position, I learned quickly that my gender transition would be an almost-impossible problem to overcome.

My masculine-sounding voice was one of the first warning flags to potential employers. Because of my years of programming experience, I received some interest from recruiters and employers. Phone interviews were a common experience, and I got plenty of those opportunities to discuss my skill set. Callbacks were a rarity, however. Most of the interviewers were polite and encouraging, stated that my skills were a good fit for their requirements, but their interest did not carry forward to second interviews or on-site visits.

Jan and I discussed the issue, and we decided that I had three options: (1) voice training to change my voice to a more feminine-sounding pitch, (2) surgery to physically modify my vocal cords to increase my pitch, and (3) leave my voice alone and continue to search, hoping that I could find an employer who would look at how my skills could apply to their company and overlook the masculine pitch of my voice.

I tried an experienced vocal coach who worked with me for several months to help me modify my voice. At the same time, I researched surgeons who had experience with modifying the male vocal cords to achieve a feminine-sounding voice. I reviewed the results of these surgeries and learned that they required a lengthy recovery and had mixed results. There were some positive results, but more that were unsatisfactory. We decided that the expense of the surgery, along with the lengthy recovery and mixed results, made this an undesirable option.

Also, I was discovering that the vocal coach route wasn't going to work, either. My voice was in the deep bass range. That made it attractive for my experience as a radio announcer and as an asset for voice recording for the embedded voice applications and voice response telephony systems I worked on. That also made it more difficult to shift the range. In addition, I was hoping that I would be able to shift between my natural voice around friends and family, who were familiar with me, while also having a more feminine voice on the telephone and in interviews with potential employers. I learned that my expectations would require considerable effort and expense to accomplish, with no promise of ever achieving desired results.

At this point, I must mention the common belief that gender surgery that modifies the genitals, along with hormone therapy, results in modification of the vocal cords and change in vocal pitch. This effect may be true for female-to-male (F2M) transsexuals who take testosterone. However, the reverse is not true for an adult male transitioning to a female (M2F). No amount of estrogen or genital surgery can reverse the effects of testosterone on the male vocal cords. During puberty, males experience an increase in testosterone, causing a thickening of the vocal cords, which lowers the vocal range. Unfortunately, the effect of estrogen does not produce a thinning of the vocal cords. Once testosterone has done its work of thickening the vocal cords, it's irreversible. That is one reason why doctors often recommend puberty blockers for prepubescent children who have identified as transgender. They prevent the irreversible effects of estrogen and testosterone until a child can attain adulthood and make their own decision about permanent transition.

In the end, I decided to leave my voice alone and hoped that potential employers would be able to accept that I was a female with a lower vocal range. Unfortunately, that never really materialized. Another reason why I decided not to attempt to modify my voice was to minimize the effects of my transition on Jan and the rest of my close friends and family. Despite the other obvious physical changes, I was still me if my voice didn't change.

I continued to have difficulty finding a job. At one point, a recruiter contacted me. She had seen my resume and was very enthusiastic about her ability to find me a job. In one of my phone interviews with her, I revealed that I was transgender and had recently transitioned. She was surprised and said she'd have to talk to one of her coworkers to see how she should handle the issue. She called back later that day and said she would not be able to help me. She believed that my transgender status would make me "unemployable." She told me I would never find a job.

That experience was quite depressing. It set me back emotionally for quite a while. As Jan and I discussed our options, we decided that I would take the time to finish my IT degree at UMass, Lowell. I had been taking night courses there for years. I sat down with one of the college advisors, and we found out that I only needed a few courses to qualify for my BS degree in IT. I had already completed several computer certificate programs at ULowell. We decided that completing the BS degree, along with my computer certificates, would give me an edge. In addition, that summer, I took a course in project management and passed the test to certify myself as a project management professional from the Project Management Institute.

About that time, September 11, 2001, happened. I was actually on my way to a class at the local Massachusetts Department of Unemployment office, listening to my car radio, when I heard the news of the first plane hitting the World Trade Center tower. I immediately turned the car around and headed back home. Like many others that day, I sat glued to the television, watching the events of that horrible day unfold. It certainly set things back. There was an effect on the economy that made my finding a job even more difficult. So, it was good that I took time off of my job hunt to complete my degree, and I received my BS-IT degree in February of 2002.

I decided that I needed a job, any kind of a job. We had just about exhausted our savings, and Jan's job wasn't enough to keep us going. I decided to modify my resume to remove all my technical experience and focus on my Microsoft Office clerical experience. Jan had earlier found a job through Kelly Services, so I sought their assistance. They put me through a battery of tests using the various Microsoft Office programs. I passed the tests with flying colors. A few days later, I got a call from Kelly offering me a job in the legal department of a company in bankruptcy. The job involved organizing their contracts in preparation for the bankruptcy resolution.

I took the job and did not discuss with them the fact that I was transgender. The company accepted me as a woman. It was there that I met Char, my first real female friend who had not known me as male. I worked as a Kelly contractor at the bankrupt company for several months. While I was there, I developed a Microsoft Access database program with a user interface that allowed anyone to enter the various contracts and the conditions of each contract that were unique to that company.

Some months later, the company decided to hire me as a permanent employee. That precipitated another step in my transition. At that time, the company confirmed my social security number with the Social Security Administration (SSA). SSA returned a notification that there was a conflict with my records. The conflict was that Social Security had my gender marker noted as male, and the company noted my gender from my driver's license as female. This situation forced a discussion with the company about my gender transition. They told me that I could not be hired until I resolved the documentation conflict.

At that time, the only way to change the gender marker in my SSA account was to submit a letter from a surgeon indicating that they had performed "irreversible sex reassignment surgery" and that I should be "legally considered female." Up to this point, I had avoided any reassignment surgery. I had not wanted to cause Jan additional distress. We had settled into life as a same-sex couple, and she had figured out how to navigate the work and family situations in which she would need to discuss me. I did not want to cause her new heartache over a complicated surgery with a lengthy, painful recovery.

In addition, sex reassignment surgery or gender confirmation surgery (GCS) was expensive and required a visit to a distant surgeon. I had a friend who went to a surgeon in Toronto to complete her surgery, and she was very satisfied with the results. The counselor we were working with was in contact with a surgeon in the western part of the country. Other contacts I had within the trans community had gone to Thailand for surgery. All of these options were expensive, and at that time, medical insurance specifically excluded GCS, which meant that we would have to come up with $20,000 to $40,000 for the surgery, plus any required travel and living costs.

I had not been willing to discuss my surgery. Such discussions are personal, and, actually, the only people who had a right to ask those questions were the people directly involved—Jan, our son, his wife, and eventually his children. Jan and I were the only people involved. We decided that I did not need full GCS. The expense, travel, and recovery times made it an impossible choice. I had heard of other M2F trans people who had completed orchiectomy surgeries that qualified as "irreversible sex reassignment surgery." Orchiectomy is a simple operation to remove the testes of a male patient. My primary doctor recommended a local urological surgeon and after contacting him, discussing what I needed to have done and the costs, we scheduled the surgery. The operation was done in March of 2005 at our local hospital on an outpatient basis. I was recovered and back to work in a couple of days.

My surgeon provided me a letter indicating that he had completed the surgery. I supplied that letter to the Records

Department at Boston City Hall, and they changed my gender on my birth certificate. I then supplied the letter and the birth certificate to the SSA, and they changed the gender marker in my SSA records, clearing the way for my hiring. I continued to work for that company until the bankruptcy process was completed in July 2006, and property and contracts were turned over to the companies that purchased the assets. I was asked to continue to work on some leftover contract issues and remained employed there for another couple of months.

While I was working on those last-minute items, I began to look for more permanent employment. I saw an ad online for a programmer experienced in a particular computer development environment for the Massachusetts Department of Workforce Development (DWD). The programming environment was one I had used in previous employment. In addition, I learned that my previous employer had developed the DWD software, but the company had gone out of business, leaving DWD with no support for a mission-critical software package. Those factors gave me an edge for the job, so I applied and had a phone interview with the supervisor who scheduled an in-person interview.

To prepare for the interview, the hiring manager sent me the Commonwealth of Massachusetts official employment application. I don't remember exactly how many pages the application was in 2006, but I remember that it was quite long. The current application is twelve pages. In any case, the one issue relating to my gender transition was the requirement that I attach a copy of my Navy discharge DD214 document. At that time, the military did not change the gender markers on their official documents, so my DD214 copies showed my male name and gender. That created a situation when I went in for my interview. While I waited with my hiring manager for the arrival of the IT department manager, the hiring manager reviewed my application. When he got to my DD214, he looked at it, then turned back to the front page with my name and gender on it, then turned back to the DD214, and then looked at me. I said that I saw an issue we needed to discuss and suggested that we wait until the IT manager arrived.

When the IT manager arrived, he sat down and immediately took charge and began to describe the position's duties. I interrupted him and said that there was an issue that we needed to discuss before we proceeded. I told them that I was transgender and had transitioned in 2001 from male to female, and that was why my US Navy records showed my male sex and name. I asked them if that would be a problem. They responded that their interest was only in my ability to maintain and develop applications for their critical software package. I told them that since I had been a programmer and manager for the company that had designed and developed the initial installation, I felt that I was fully qualified to manage their applications. They agreed that if that was true, then we would have no issues with my personal situation.

I worked for the DWD from October 2006 through December 2012, when I took an early retirement package and my state pension. The pension was based on the buyback of my four years of state teaching credit, along with my four years of Navy credit. I had announced in early October that I was planning on retiring at the end of 2012. Jan and I discussed our living situation in retirement and decided that we could not continue to live in our house in Massachusetts. Our mortgage would be difficult for us to manage with only our social security and pension.

Jan wanted to move back to the Midwest to be closer to her mother and to move farther south to avoid the cold weather and heavy snows of New England winters. While discussing our options, I noticed a posting on LinkedIn from a manager of Humana in Louisville. The posting was for a position similar to the type of positions I held at the DWD and other technology companies for whom I had worked. I called Jan and asked her if she'd like to move to Louisville, Kentucky. She responded that she would if I was willing to come along. I told her about the job posting, and after we discussed it, we decided that I would apply for the position and see where the process would take us.

I submitted my application and had several phone interviews. During the first interview, I discussed my transition, and they assured me that Humana was a very diverse company with an active LGBT employee group. Jan and I were invited to travel to Louisville for on-site interviews and to visit the city and look at potential moving options. We were flown out to Louisville and stayed in the historic Seelbach Hilton Hotel. The next morning, we were met by representatives of the Humana LGBT group to discuss our concerns. Kentucky is known to be a particularly conservative state, but we were assured that Louisville was "a blue enclave in a red state." That was encouraging. I met with the managers and other people I would be working with, while Jan met with a real estate agent who took her on a tour of Louisville neighborhoods.

When we returned to Massachusetts, I received an offer from Humana that included the cost of the move, temporary housing, and a real estate agent to help us find permanent housing. We decided to accept the offer. I was to start my new position at Humana in late February 2013. I retired from DWD on December 31, 2012, and after New Year's, hired two organizers to assist me with preparing for the move. We contacted a disposal company to get a large dumpster for disposing of items we no longer needed. We filled up the first dumpster in one week and replaced it with another. We had accumulated a lot of "junk" over twenty-nine years in the same house. We also donated clothes and unneeded furniture and appliances to various charities.

In mid-January 2013, Jan and I flew out to Louisville for a weekend house-hunting trip. On Saturday, our real estate agent drove us around to look at various properties that looked interesting. The last property we looked at was a "patio home" in a condo development in Jeffersontown, Kentucky, a suburb south of Louisville. We really liked the layout of the condo. It was all on a single floor, which was important because Jan had problems with both knees and had difficulty going up and down stairs. We were told that there was an open house scheduled for that condo the next day, so we decided to put in an offer right away after going back to our hotel. We called our agent, and she came up to our hotel room that evening and put together our offer. Eventually, our offer was accepted.

On February 26, 2013, we left Massachusetts for Louisville with a U-Haul trailer and two very unhappy cats. We stayed in temporary housing in the Crowne Springs complex in Eastern Louisville from February 27 until we could close on our new property in Louisville. Our household goods were delivered in March. We hired an organizer to help Jan get unpacked while I went to work at one of the Humana offices in downtown Louisville.

We enjoyed our stay in Louisville. Humana was a great company to work for, and my managers and coworkers in Louisville and my developer teams in India were very accepting. Humana encouraged us to work from home when we needed to and allowed me to work from Maine during the summers while we stayed in our camper there at a campground. The winters were mild with little snow (for a native New Englander), and when the hot and humid summers arrived, we abandoned Louisville for Maine. Things were going well.

Jan retired while we were in Kentucky and worked on genealogy, researching her ancestors on both her father's and mother's sides. Then age hit, and her knees became an issue that needed surgery. She had one knee replaced early in 2014 by an orthopedic surgeon. It took Jan several months to recover, and during that time, I worked from home most of the time.

In October of 2015, I left Humana. I had decided during our summer in Maine that I'd had enough of working. I was worn out and gave my notice to Humana that I was leaving. My retirement gave Jan and me more time to spend together and go to concerts and travel.

Jan's Battle with Cancer

In April of 2010, we received the news that Jan had cancer. Jan had gone to our doctor for her annual checkup, and at the end, she asked the doctor to look at her right breast. She had noted some changes in it over the past months. The doctor looked at it and asked her about the changes. Jan told her that it had been itchy, and she had noticed some seepage from the nipple. They couldn't feel any lumps, but the doctor thought that Jan should have a biopsy to make sure. Jan didn't tell me about the doctor's diagnosis at first. She thought she could have the biopsy, and then if anything was found, tell me about the results. A few days later, however, she decided to tell me about the doctor's concerns and the scheduled biopsy.

We had a surgeon we were familiar with do the biopsy, and he found what our doctor had suspected; Jan had inflammatory breast cancer (IBC). We were to find out that IBC is the rarest and most virulent type of breast cancer and is most often misdiagnosed as mastitis. This delay in proper diagnosis can be deadly since it is also a fast-growing cancer. IBC is unique in that a mammogram cannot diagnose it. *WebMD* describes IBC as "a rare and aggressive form of breast cancer that often appears as a rash or an irritated area of skin. It blocks the lymph vessels in the skin of your breast. Inflammatory breast cancer may not show up on a mammogram or ultrasound and is often misdiagnosed as an infection. By the time it's diagnosed, it usually has grown into the skin of your breast. Sometimes, it has already spread to other parts of the body, too."[15] We were so fortunate that our doctor had experience with IBC. She sent Jan for a biopsy immediately, so she avoided the delay in diagnosis that increased the seriousness of the cancer.

WebMD characterizes this type of cancer as usually occurring in one of three stages:

- Stage IIIB: All inflammatory breast cancers start in this stage since they involve the skin of your breast.

- Stage IIIC: This cancer has spread to lymph nodes around your collarbone or inside your chest.

- Stage IV: The cancer has spread outside your breast and nearby lymph nodes to other parts of your body.

WebMD also notes that the usual diagnosis is Stage III and that the survival rate for that diagnosis is typically in the range of five years.[15]

We met with an oncologist in our local hospital, and she told us that it was probably already at stage IV, which meant that it was almost terminal. We discussed this with our son, and he was talking with some friends at work about it. The wife of one of those friends worked at Dana Farber Cancer Institute (DFCI) in Boston, a world-renowned cancer treatment facility. She arranged for an appointment for Jan with a specialist at DFCI, and we were there within a couple of days. The specialist was the director of the research group

---

[15] "https://www.webmd.com/breast-cancer/inflammatory-breast-cancer

for IBC there at DFCI—Dr. Beth Overmoyer—Dr. O, as Jan used to call her.

Dr. O sat with us and immediately told us she saw no reason for a stage IV diagnosis. It was stage III. She explained to us what IBC was, drawing diagrams on a blank sheet of paper. She described the treatment regimen she would recommend. We proceeded with her plan, and Jan embarked on her battle to subdue IBC. It involved a lengthy process of chemotherapy followed by a complete right-breast mastectomy, including the removal of twenty-one lymph nodes under her right armpit. A regimen of radiation therapy followed that.

The whole process took almost a year, with rest periods between each treatment portion, to allow Jan's body to recover. By March of 2011, she had completed her treatment and was beginning to recover. I was at her side for each chemo session and in the waiting room during her mastectomy surgery. Since her radiation sessions were daily, I could not take enough time off work to be with her for all those sessions. The radiation was the worst part of the whole treatment process. It was as if she had the worst sunburn ever. I helped her with that by applying the ointment she was prescribed to heal the intense burns. She participated in a short clinical trial following the conclusion of her radiation treatment. This trial involved several vaccine injections developed from the cancer cells removed from her breast during surgery. Following that trial, Jan was declared "cancer-free" or "no evidence of disease" (NED). Our lives began to return to some semblance of post-cancer normalcy.

In April of 2017, our doctor in Louisville was on leave to care for her father, who was in the last stages of his battle with cancer. Jan was having some physical problems, and one of the other doctors in the practice saw her and ordered tests. Our regular doctor called into the office on a weekend and noticed the tests that the other doctor had ordered for Jan. She reviewed the results and was concerned about the buildup of fluid in one of Jan's lungs. She called us on a Sunday afternoon to discuss with Jan her concerns and recommended more tests be done.

Several tests and more specialists later, we were notified that Jan's IBC had metastasized to some lymph nodes near her right lung. We decided that we wanted Jan's oncologist at Dana Farber Cancer Institute (DFCI) in Boston to give us a second opinion. We called Dr. Overmoyer, and Jan had an appointment the next Tuesday. We drove up to Boston that weekend. Jan and I met with Dr. O, and she confirmed the diagnosis. We decided that we would let Dr. O manage Jan's treatment there at DFCI. We drove back to Louisville, packed for our summer in Maine, put the cats in the car, and drove to Maine to spend the summer there.

Jan was on a three-week schedule for her treatments. On Monday, she would get her treatment; then, Monday a week later, she would get another treatment, followed the next Monday by a week off. We drove down to Boston from Maine for the treatments.

When it was time for the campground to close in the fall, we had a decision to make. How could we continue her treatments in Louisville? Since Jan was in a clinical trial, she was required to be treated in Boston, or she would have to stop her treatment. We decided that we could make the trip up to Boston once every three weeks but that we needed to find someplace to stay for the week between the two treatments. The pastor at our church suggested that we could use a bedroom that they could set up in the parsonage living room, and we could stay there on our trips to Dana Farber. We were so thankful for that hospitality. Without that, we would have had to either end Jan's treatment at DFCI or pay for hotel rooms for weeks at a time—an expensive proposition far beyond our financial ability.

We returned to Louisville in the fall of 2017 and began our winter road trips back and forth between Louisville and Boston. Each trip up and returning, we stayed overnight in Buffalo, New York, at a hotel near the Buffalo Airport. The staff there quickly learned our situation and were gracious and caring. There were times when Jan was very sick, and the staff at the hotel would get a wheelchair for her and help get her to our room. They gave us the same room almost every time. It had a roll-in shower so Jan could have her shower without having to climb into a tub.

In the spring of 2018, we went back to our camp in Maine for the summer, which made our weekly trips to Dana Farber simpler. We had a good summer, but it became clearer that the treatments were not making much progress. At the end of the summer, Dr. Overmoyer told us that there were no more clinical trials that Jan qualified for and that the team had decided it would be best for Jan to be put on what was termed as a "standard of care." In other words, it was what patients were given who could not receive any benefit from available clinical trials. We were told that Jan could receive treatment from doctors in Louisville.

We wanted Dr. O to continue monitoring her treatment progress; we had found the oncologists in Louisville unco-operative when it came to allowing other doctors to manage their patient's treatment regimens. We decided to use an oncologist from Cleveland Clinic, a day's ride from Louisville, to manage the testing and evaluation process. Dr. O had worked at Cleveland Clinic, and the oncologist she chose there was a friend and colleague of long-standing. We felt comfortable with Louisville Cancer Clinic administering the treatment, Cleveland Clinic doing the testing and evaluation of progress, and Dr. O overseeing the whole process.

During our years in Louisville, Jan began to have increased trouble swallowing food. Her gastroenterologist in Louisville diagnosed her with achalasia. This is a condition in which the lower esophageal muscles cannot relax, which causes the inability to get food down to the stomach, so swallowed food comes back up. Jan was told that there was no reliable treatment for this condition. Doctors agreed that Jan's radiation treatment probably caused it during her first bout with cancer. Apparently, the muscle was weakened by the intense radiation she had received in her chest and neck area.

In the winter of 2018, Jan had a serious problem with her achalasia while in Louisville. She was unable to keep any food down for several weeks. We contacted her gastroenterologist, and set an appointment a couple of weeks away. When we finally got to the doctor's office on the day of the appointment, she had not been able to keep solid food down for almost a month. When Jan went to the reception desk to let them know she was there for her appointment, the receptionist told her that her doctor was not in and no other doctor was available to see her. They offered to make another appointment several weeks away. I went ballistic. I was upset that the office would treat Jan so callously. I asked the receptionist how they expected her to live without solid food. We received no other alternative.

Jan decided to call Dr. Overmoyer at Dana Farber for advice. Dr. O set up an appointment with one of the gastroenterologists at Brigham and Women's Hospital (BWH), so we drove back up there. Jan was given a treatment in which Botox is injected into the lower esophageal muscle to relax it. She was told that the effects were temporary. This condition continued to be a problem, and Jan weakened steadily. She was fighting cancer with a body weakened by a lack of good nourishment. Jan remained in Brigham and Women's Hospital for a few days and then went to a rehab center north of Boston.

While Jan was there, since the campground in Maine had opened for the season, I headed home to Louisville to pack up what we would need for the summer, loaded the cats in the car, and headed back to Maine. I stopped at the rehab center on the way up, and Jan came out to the car to see the cats.

I traveled down to the rehab center almost every day to spend time with Jan. She was released in late June, and we went up to Maine and relaxed. It was clear that she had not been able to eat properly at the rehab center and that she was having more problems keeping food down. Fortunately, our son, daughter-in-law, and the grandchildren were vacationing in Sebago during the Fourth of July week. They were able to come to our campground and visit with Jan for part of a day.

The week following, Jan had an appointment at DFCI for treatment. When we got into the infusion room, we found out that Dr. O was waiting for us. She asked us how Jan was doing. I told her that Jan had been having more difficulty keeping food down and was getting weaker. Dr. O suggested that another Botox treatment on the lower esophageal muscle would help. Jan was admitted to BWH and scheduled for the procedure. Before the procedure, I was invited into the surgery suite so that we could both talk to the surgeon. He suggested that the next time Jan needed this procedure, we could contact his office directly and that it could be done on an outpatient basis. We agreed to this, although I could tell that Jan was discouraged at the thought of having to go through this process, possibly monthly, for the rest of her life.

Following the procedure, Jan was sent back to her hospital room for recovery. It was becoming clear that Jan was getting weaker. We had several conversations with the hospice team at BWH and with Dr. O. We decided to move back to New England, so I contacted our real estate agent in Louisville. She helped me contact an agent who covered Maine and New Hampshire, and I started getting our condo in Louisville ready to sell and looking in New England for someplace to move.

On July 20, our son and his family came to the hospital to visit Jan. It was clear to all of us that she was nearing the end of her journey. Our son made a call to Jan's stepsister, Jody, and the two of them talked for a while. On the next day, Sunday, some of the pastors who knew us visited and prayed with us. It was becoming evident to me that Jan was at peace and was ready to make the transition.

On Monday, our son and I sat with her most of the day. She was not speaking or conscious that day. I was with her Tuesday, July 23. She was comatose during the day and having breathing problems. At about 1:15 p.m., she took a deep sigh and breath and stopped breathing. I called the nurse, and she came in and confirmed that her heart had stopped. It was heartbreaking. We had been together and loved each other since Saturday, June 24, 1961—just about fifty-eight years and one month. We had been married since November 28, 1964—four months short of fifty-five years—and been through all the usual turmoil of life and then some. Now the focus of my life was gone.

The Perils of Gender Transition

As I mentioned earlier, Jan and I were active in trans support groups for several years, and we had observed the effects of gender transition in the lives of many of our friends. I've never understood the idea that some people have that a person chooses to be transgender. Anyone with that idea is certainly not familiar with the high costs of being identified as trans.

The most dangerous cost of transition is the likelihood of loss of life. Each year on November 20, the trans community takes time to mourn those of our number who have lost their lives to transphobic violence. That number grows larger and larger. In recent years the lives lost in the US have come predominantly from the African-American trans community. However, regardless of our ethnicity, it's physically dangerous to be trans for any of us.

Even I experienced an episode of sexual harassment. It occurred before I officially transitioned, when I was out on Halloween night with Jan and a group of our Tiffany friends. I had to go to the restroom at a club we were visiting. I felt uncomfortable going to the ladies' room because I had not yet transitioned, and I suspected that I would be seen as a male in the ladies' room, particularly since this was Halloween. Several of my Tiffany friends decided to use the ladies' room, and one was removed from the club for being in the wrong restroom. When I entered the men's room, I went into a stall and completed my task. I then left the stall and approached a sink to wash up. A young man at another sink commented on my appearance and made a snide remark. Then he commented on my breasts and said, "Hey, those look better than my girlfriends!" and grabbed my breast and squeezed. I pulled away and said, "I'm sorry for you!" and left. That experience was scary, and I certainly did not experience the level of abuse of many women, but it gave me a small inkling of what it felt like to be treated as an object, to be "manhandled" at will.

Not only is it the risk of being attacked physically and injured or killed, but also it's the danger that we internalize society's fear and hatred and succumb to suicide. That solution is far too common among trans persons. In 2020 the Trevor Project released a survey of over 40,000 LGBTQ youth ages thirteen to twenty-four that concluded "40% of LGBTQ respondents seriously considered attempting suicide in the past twelve months, with more than half (52%) of transgender and nonbinary youth having seriously considered suicide."[16] Unfortunately, it's difficult to identify the number of suicides that occur due to a person's gender identity struggles. The danger of suicide is not limited to youth alone. In August 2015, the National Center for Transgender Equality (NCTE) launched the US Transgender Survey (USTS) of almost 28,000 respondents which "found that 81.7 percent of respondents reported ever seriously thinking about suicide in their lifetimes, while 48.3 percent had done so in the past year. In regard to suicide attempts, 40.4 percent reported attempting suicide at some point in their lifetimes, and 7.3

---

[16] https://www.thetrevorproject.org/survey-2020/?section =Introduction

percent reported attempting suicide in the past year."[17] One of Jan's strongest objections to my transition was her fear for my physical safety.

Wikipedia tells the story of Leelah Alcorn, whose suicide in December 2014 attracted worldwide media attention:

Leelah Alcorn…was an American transgender girl whose suicide attracted international attention; she had posted a suicide note to her Tumblr blog about societal standards affecting transgender people and expressing the hope that her death would create a dialogue about discrimination, abuse, and lack of support for transgender people.

Born and raised in Kings Mills, Ohio, Alcorn was assigned male at birth and grew up in a family affiliated with the Church of Christ movement. At age fourteen, she came out as transgender to her parents, Carla and Doug Alcorn, who refused to accept her female gender identity. When she was sixteen, they denied her request to undergo transition treatment, instead sending her to Christian-based conversion therapy with the intention of convincing her to reject her gender identity and accept her gender as assigned at birth. After she revealed her attraction toward males to her classmates, her parents removed her from school and revoked her access to social media.

In her note, she stated her intention to end her life, commenting:

---

[17] Herman, Jody L., Brown, Taylor N.T., and Haas, Ann P., "Suicide Thoughts and Attempts Among Transgender Adults," Findings from the 2015 US Transgender Survey, p. 1; https://escholarship.org/uc/item/1812g3hm

"I have decided I've had enough. I'm never going to transition successfully, even when I move out. I'm never going to be happy with the way I look or sound. I'm never going to have enough friends to satisfy me. I'm never going to have enough love to satisfy me. I'm never going to find a man who loves me. I'm never going to be happy. Either I live the rest of my life as a lonely man who wishes he were a woman, or I live my life as a lonelier woman who hates herself. There's no winning. There's no way out. I'm sad enough already. I don't need my life to get any worse. People say "it gets better," but that isn't true in my case. It gets worse. Each day I get worse. That's the gist of it, that's why I feel like killing myself. Sorry if that's not a good enough reason for you; it's good enough for me."

In the early morning of December 28, 2014, police informed news sources that she had been walking along Interstate 71 near Union Township when she was struck by a semi-trailer just before 2:30 a.m., near the South Lebanon exit. She died at the scene. It is believed that Alcorn walked three to four miles from her parents' Kings Mill house before being struck.[18]

The sad thing about this incident is that it is far too common. The only uncommon thing about this incident is the notoriety it attracted. Because Leelah had published her suicide note on the Internet, it attracted wide attention from the media, and many activists were very critical of her parents' position.

Often the trans person's thoughts of suicide are minimized by friends and family. Unfortunately, they are very real. I reached that point many times in my life, and that usually motivated me to talk to counselors. It was clear to both

---

[18] https://en.wikipedia.org/wiki/Leelah_Alcorn.

Jan and me, though, when we had our discussions about my transition in the late 1990s, that I had reached the end of my ability to manage the conflict raging in me and that it was either transition or suicide. I'm sure that others of our family and relatives did not comprehend that point and felt that my desire to transition was selfish and thoughtless. It was anything but. One of the main reasons I was trying to avoid any permanent solution that would end my life was because I knew what that would do to Jan. We later talked about how my transition had resolved my gender conflict but also permitted me to be with Jan as her caregiver through cancer treatments, knee surgeries, and eating disorders.

The second most prominent issue in my transition was the loss of family and friends. My first question in our discussions about my transition was if Jan would remain with me. I could not have survived if she had left me. As I noted earlier, she responded, "As of today, I'm going to remain. I don't want to have to train another partner." Our experience before and after my transition was that almost all spouses of trans people end their relationship. We counseled many couples struggling with the decision to transition. Almost always, the wife responded that she had married a man and could not remain married if he transitioned into a woman. On the other hand, the trans person's response usually was that they had to complete the transition process they had longed for and that any compromise due to their wife's feelings was unacceptable. This approach created an impossible situation for both persons and ultimately ended in separation and eventual divorce.

We did meet a (very) few couples who remained together during the transition. I mentioned before, one couple we met in a support group was Anne and Nancy. They became our lifelong friends, and Nancy and Jan could help each other over the many rough spots.

It's not just life partners that trans people risk losing, although they are usually the most important. It's parents, siblings, children, and other extended family members that often reject the trans person. For a young person—teen and young adult—struggling with their gender identity, their parents and siblings are most important. Often, when young people tell their parents of their struggle, their feelings are minimized, and if they persist, they must leave home. Such situations often drive the children to the streets and too often into sex work, which is dangerous beyond words. In other cases, like Leelah Alcorn, they are driven to suicide.

The threat of suicide was certainly an element of my transition—my desire to remove the turmoil I had experienced throughout my life. However, I had gone through the struggle for over thirty-five years of marriage and raising a son. I focused on what was best for my family and attempted to minimize the effects of gender confusion on myself. I was nearing the end stage of my life. Our son had grown up to be a fine person, had completed college and graduate school, had a good job, and was married and starting a family of his own. He let us know in no uncertain terms that he did not need or want our input and support. That was appropriate given his stage of life.

So, it came down to a decision between Jan and me. Jan understood my struggles. She was the only one who really had a grasp of what I had gone through. She also had come to understand that this was a condition that I was born with. It was not a mistake that God had made. It was a normal occurrence within the human experience. There have been trans people throughout history. Even the Bible notes the condition in what it calls "eunuchs." In Matthew 19:12, Jesus is quoted as saying, "For there are eunuchs who were born that way, and there are eunuchs who have been made eunuchs by others—and there are those who choose to live like eunuchs for the sake of the kingdom of heaven. The one who can accept this should accept it."

The most difficult loss we experienced was that of our son and the grandchildren. He had begun to separate his life from us, but my transition marked an almost complete break. It took several years for us to work through the separation. At one point, our son chose a counselor through his company health insurance plan who would meet with us to see if we could reach some accommodation. We had a few sessions before I broke off the attempt. The counselor was not familiar with transgender issues and was not sympathetic, and we just were not making any progress toward reconciliation. I thought of the struggles Jan and I had experienced through the years, attempting to make his life as free from my gender identity issues as possible so that he could have a "normal" life, and since he was moving on with his life, we needed to do so also.

The most difficult part was our isolation from our grandchildren. One Christmas, we had to drop off on their front porch our presents for the grandkids. We were never allowed to watch any of the grandkids' school activities. Sports events and other activities were off-limits for us. They told us that my presence might embarrass the children and precipitate a conflict with other parents or children. We were eventually allowed to see the grandchildren only by visiting their home. They only visited our house, which was about a twenty-minute drive from theirs, a couple of times over the fifteen years or so as the grandchildren matured. At one point, they told Jan that she was welcome to attend the children's activities without me. She responded that if I were not welcome to attend, she would not either.

Another issue that arose was the celebration of Father's Day. One time we were visiting, and they told us that they would no longer celebrate Father's Day since I was no longer male and could not be a father. My position was that I would always be our son's father, regardless of whatever form I took. I told them that I felt that history and genetics could not be denied. They were adamant, however, that they would not celebrate Father's Day in the future. They continued to celebrate Mother's Day, and our son sent cards and called Jan each Mother's Day. Each Father's Day, Jan gave me a card, and we celebrated the fact that we had brought him into the world, but it was a yearly reminder of the brokenness of our relationship with our son.

We also lost the connection to my birth mother and her family. As I mentioned earlier in this book, during our move to Massachusetts in 1983, I discovered the information about my adoption in my father's desk. The letter from his lawyer gave my birth mother's name and her location at that time. I decided to put off trying to locate my birth family until after we had completed our move and were settled. In 1989, I finally contacted an adoption search agency, and they located my birth mother. I wrote her a letter, and we made contact.

My birth mother had married twice and had had five other children after me, one from her first marriage and four from her existing marriage. Since two of her children had died in separate accidents in 1981, there were three children—two sisters and a brother—along with her husband whom I met. My mother's husband passed away late in 1992. However, between 1989 and 2001, the year I transitioned, Jan and I and our son and his family became a part of their family.

We were invited to various family celebrations and holiday get-togethers.

When we made the decision that I would transition, Jan and I met with my birth mother's family. It was clear that they were not ready to accept my transition. My entry into the family had been difficult enough to deal with, but the gender transition was too much. We agreed at that point that we would go our separate ways. When my mother passed away in 2009, it was made clear that I was not welcome at her funeral. Our son and daughter-in-law did attend. Jan and I have maintained contact with one of my mother's grandchildren. Other than that, the relationships we established during those years were broken.

The other types of relationships that were difficult to maintain were the friends we had made throughout our lives and our work relationships. Many of those were transitory, and as happens with many lifetime relationships, we had lost contact or were living in a different area. It was not necessary to track them down for a gender reveal. As long as there was no physical contact with them, my gender transition was not an issue. Once, a friend from one of my former workplaces showed up unannounced at our front door for a visit. It created a difficult situation, but we decided not to say anything. We just welcomed him and had a good conversation; he left after a short time.

I certainly wish Jan were still here to recount her experiences at work and with her extended family. In all cases involving Jan's friends or family, I deferred to her decision about what and when to reveal my transition. Most of the time at work, she referred to me as her husband or spouse. Usually, at each workplace, she would have a close friend to confide in, one who knew about the transition. It was a more difficult situation with her family. Jan's stepfather died in 1998, and her father died in 2008, both of them in Ohio. Neither of them or any of Jan's other relatives knew about my transition, as far as we knew.

Because Jan's father's death occurred seven years post-transition, my attendance at his funeral presented an issue. I decided that it would be easiest for Jan if I attended dressed in male clothes. Not only was it difficult to even think about reverting to male clothes, but I had discarded almost all of them. That meant I had to purchase a suit, shirts, shoes, and slacks for the funeral and other associated events. Frankly, that experience was most difficult and very nerve-racking, but in a way, it confirmed that my decision to transition was the right one. I don't know if any of Jan's relatives were aware of the changes that had occurred in me, but at any rate, I was able to support Jan in her grieving, and I survived the reversion process.

Jan had not told her mother or her stepsiblings of my transition. In 2005 we decided to reveal my transition to Jan's mother. She was very angry at our revelation, and, after, she and Jan had several conversations in which she expressed her opinion that I was sinning and would be condemned to hell. In addition, she told Jan that I would not be permitted to attend her funeral. These statements were very distressing to Jan, and they motivated me to write her mother. The letter expressing my feelings is attached as an addendum to this book. It may serve as an illustration of some of the arguments used for and against gender identity issues. It also is an example of Jan's turmoil as a result of her mother's rejection.

Eventually, her mother came around and accepted me after one of Jan's stepsisters, who lived with her mother, did some Internet investigation and realized that my transition was not to be condemned. I was welcomed at Jan's stepsister's funeral in 2011 and her mother's funeral in 2018.

Another element that adds difficulty to transitioning is the problem of finding medical care. First, finding a regular primary care physician (PCP) can be difficult. When Jan was with me, I was fortunate that I didn't have any issues with our doctors. When I transitioned, the PCP we had at that time was supportive and understanding. I had a counselor who referred me to an endocrinologist who was supportive and regularly treated transitioning patients. I had a history of having blood clots, so there was concern that the side effects of taking estrogen, which was known as a clotting enhancer, could be dangerous. As a result, I was referred to a hematologist who did some tests. She concluded that there would be no additional danger if the estrogen and clotting factors were regularly monitored.

Unfortunately, a few years into my estrogen treatment, the supplier of the estrogen I was using changed, and so did the dosage. I was taking the estrogen by regular injections, and the syringes I was using made it difficult to gauge the new dosage. The result was that I overdosed on estrogen for several months, which resulted in my getting some clots. My endo was angry and dropped me as a patient. I was treated for the clotting and recovered without an issue. I consulted another endocrinologist and decided that I had already seen the full feminizing effects of the estrogen treatment. I was also past the age of menopause, when most women experience the cessation of estrogen production. So, I decided that I would stop all estrogen treatments. However, I will take medication to treat the risk of clotting for the rest of my life.

When we moved to Louisville, Kentucky, in 2013, we had some difficulty finding a PCP, but finally were able to get a doctor who was understanding and supportive. She was one of the most conscientious doctors we had known. Her vigilance, as I mentioned previously, was responsible for catching the recurrence of Jan's cancer. I will always be grateful to her for the dedication she showed that resulted in Jan's getting treated for the metastasis of her cancer.

When I moved back to New England after Jan's passing, I encountered problems finding a new doctor in my area. During 2020, at the height of the COVID-19 pandemic, many doctors in my area were not accepting new patients. I had some vision issues, so I visited an eye doctor for new glasses. One morning I noticed a change in my field of vision. My left-side peripheral vision was pretty much gone. I called the eye doctor who evaluated me, and she felt that I might have experienced a mild stroke. She told me to see a primary care doctor immediately so that the effects of the stroke could be evaluated. In the same medical facility, I had previously found a nurse practitioner who would take me as a patient. I had already made an appointment that, at that time, was several weeks away. The eye doctor called the NP's office and arranged for an appointment in a couple of days. She also arranged for an MRI study to be done the morning of the NP appointment. I had received the new patient packet for my pending visit with the NP, so I quickly filled it out (including my transition history and associated surgeries) and dropped it off after I visited the MRI center.

I took some relaxant medication before the scheduled MRI. Unfortunately, I was unable have the MRI done that day, and when I got back home, while waiting for my afternoon appointment with the NP, I fell asleep. I woke up five minutes before my appointment time. The NP's office was only fifteen minutes from my house, so I quickly got in my car and drove toward the office. On the way, five minutes after

I was due at the office, I called on my cell phone to let them know I was on my way. The office staff told me that since I didn't arrive on time, my appointment had been canceled, and the office told me that the next available appointment would be in five months. I felt sure that the cancellation and the lengthy reschedule time was because they had seen my transition history and didn't want to treat me.

With the help of the eye doctor's staff, it took me several more weeks to find a permanent primary care doctor, and the vision was resolved, but I felt that this incident was a clear example of discrimination. Trump promised to be a supporter of the LGBTQI community. Despite this promise, the Trump administration did everything possible to make it difficult for LGBT folks to get medical treatment. He signed an executive order that implemented a "conscience" rule that allowed doctors to refuse to treat people, even in the case of a medical emergency, if doing so violated their sincerely held religious beliefs. Judges blocked the implementation of the rule. Still, it would not be until President Biden that the policy was reversed and Obamacare guidance was reinstated and expanded to include a Supreme Court ruling that sex discrimination includes sexual orientation and gender identity.

I was finally able to get the MRI done, and the results were evaluated by my eye doctor, a neurologist, and my new primary care doctor. The consensus was that I had experienced a mild stoke that would continue to limit some of my left-side peripheral vision.

Not only is it difficult to get the standard medical treatment, it's also more difficult to get specific treatment for gender identity issues. Surgeons who will do gender confirmation surgery for both male-to-female and female-to-male patients are limited in number. Often, trans people have to travel across the country or even out of the country to find a surgeon trained in the difficult surgeries that must be done. Also, until recently, insurance companies did not pay for the required surgeries. Most insurance policies specifically excluded any treatment, including surgery, to change gender. Now, Obamacare and most commercial insurance policies are allowing such treatment to be paid.

One thing that I ran into, which would still be an issue today, is most doctors' reluctance to perform surgery on overweight individuals like me. In addition, my clotting issues make any surgery more dangerous. Because of these issues, I would not be able to get full gender confirmation surgery, and my options are limited. As mentioned in a previous chapter, I was able to find a surgeon in the New England area who was willing to do a limited surgical procedure that qualified as "irreversible sex reassignment surgery." That surgery was acceptable to Jan, and it allowed me to get my birth-certificate gender changed and other records updated to indicate my correct gender.

The difficulties of finding routine medical treatment, the issues with hormone treatment, the scarcity of surgeons, and problematic insurance coverage are major problems for the trans community, particularly young trans people who lack parental support and low-income persons who experience gender identity issues. Unfortunately, many trans people choose to self-medicate, using hormones from sources that the FDA has not approved. It's not easy being trans, and no one would voluntarily choose this life path.

One of the most difficult elements of transitioning is finding employment. This is particularly a problem for trans people because so much of the transition involves paying for services. Without a job and insurance, it's almost impossible to successfully and safely complete the transition. As I mentioned earlier, I ran into a recruiter who told me that my gender transition made me unemployable. It took over two years for me to find employment after my transition. Then, it required that I minimize my technical skills on my resume and look for a clerical position (at clerical salary) using a temp agency. I was accepted as a female at the company where I worked and was able to perform my tasks and provide additional value by using my technical skills. I became a valued employee and was hired on a permanent basis. Eventually, I was able to work at the Massachusetts Department of Workforce Development and at Humana, where I was hired based on my full technical experience and where I was open about my transition with both employers.

Even in an accepting environment, trans people can encounter discrimination. Companies need to know that, even though they may develop anti-discrimination policies for hiring, existing employees may have homophobic or transphobic feelings. By utilizing whisper campaigns to denigrate the trans persons' skills and value to the company, those employees may work to undermine the ability of the trans person to function. Companies must let all their employees know that discrimination will not be tolerated from any source. It's often difficult to prove that discrimination occurs, as most women understand from years of employment discrimination and sexual harassment.

When I worked for Massachusetts DWD, I experienced one episode of discrimination. My manager called me into his office one day and told me some employees had found a link on the Internet that showed me at the United Methodist General Conference, discussing transgender issues at a media session. The link was being passed around among the employees. He asked me how I wanted the issue handled. Since my gender transition had not been discussed with all the employees, I decided that first I needed to discuss it with the employees in my department so that they would be aware of my situation and have the opportunity to ask any questions. My coworkers expressed acceptance, and one told me, "If anyone gives you any problems, let me know, and I'll take care of them."

One issue I ran into at both DWD and Humana was that, although both places did have nondiscrimination policies, they had not carried those policies into their business practices. At DWD, I encouraged the department to develop policies to aid LGBTQI workers in job hunting. I felt that they were in an ideal position to assist those workers over the hurdles they would encounter finding employment due to their gender identity or sexual orientation. I also felt that they could assist in developing and encouraging anti-discrimination policies for companies in the Commonwealth. Unfortunately, I was not able to make any headway in either area while I was there.

I ran into similar issues while I was at Humana. Since their main business was medical coverage, I tried to encourage Humana to work with employers to remove existing limitations in medical insurance coverage for transgender patients. I did get an opportunity to educate them about some of the inadequacies of medical coverage for normal procedures that might need to be done, which would not be usual for non-trans persons. For example, insurance companies regularly deny coverage for PSA tests for male-to-female patients. Since the PSA test is normally performed only on males, anyone designated as female would be denied coverage. In one instance early in my transition, my doctor ordered a PSA test, and the nurse administering the test was not allowed to enter the test in my digital order until she changed my gender designation to male. It took me months to reverse that change in my records. Fortunately, Humana was open to developing policies that would eliminate this issue.

Being Transgender in the 21st Century

Much has changed about being trans since I first became aware of the issue. As I grew up in the last half of the twentieth century, there was almost no information about gender identity issues. My preteen and teenage years were a time of great confusion. I had no idea what was going on in my life. I just knew that I wished I were a girl and that wearing female clothing gave me a feeling of release from the internal conflict. My first inkling of what was going on occurred, as I mentioned previously, when Christine Jorgensen's transition became public in the early 1950s. While that information was the start of my understanding of where I fit, it was no help because the responses of the public and my parents to the information were a lesson in intolerance. Based on those reactions, I could not see a way to find a solution to my conflict.

When Jan and I were married, neither of us had any solution other than that we felt that together we could manage whatever conflict we encountered. Jan had less information than I had about the issue. When circumstances forced me to reveal my cross-dressing to her, all I could say was that dressing in women's clothing calmed the conflict I felt. We managed the issue for years as I completed college and began working and raising our son. All the while, we kept our "secret" between the two of us, doing our best to try to understand and deal with the feelings. We were both very conflicted.

At one point in the midseventies, I went to the library at the University of Cincinnati, looking for references about what I was feeling. In that large college library, I found just one book in the psychology section that discussed gender conflicts in a portion of one page, identifying them as a sub-category of homosexuality, which was not how I identified. Jan and I didn't understand what was going on, and Jan resented this intrusion into our lives. I was suppressing the feelings, and I didn't act upon them sometimes for months at a time. However, it was becoming clear that suppressing the feelings was not a solution; it was only driving me closer to a final resolution that would affect all of us—my suicide. Those feelings were what drove me to counseling.

Counselors in the '70s didn't have much information about the conflict I was experiencing. Later, Jan and I joked that I was training the counselors about what being transgender meant. One counselor sent me to a psychiatrist who diag-nosed me as a "transvestite." That was a term my father had used when he questioned me about my cross-dressing when I was a teenager. We know now that the term *transvestite* as it was applied then referred to cross-dressing only and did not contemplate the transexual experience. After we moved back to the Boston area and became involved in Tiffany Club, we met with counselors who were more familiar with the range of experiences. Then the term *transgender* was used to describe a range of cross-gender experiences, and we began to understand where I fit.

Unfortunately, I had to go through over fifty years of con-fusion before we came to a solution. Not only did I have struggles, but I dragged a wife and a child into my confusion. Today, children have available much more information as they grow up. As they begin to become aware at a young age of their feelings of being the wrong gender, they and their parents have information available on the Internet. Also, trained gender counselors and several gender clinics around the country are available to help the families identify if the feelings constitute a real cross-gender experience or simple childhood experimentation. It takes a trained clinician to correctly identify the best way to handle the feelings the child is experiencing.

For preteens who have gone through clinical evaluation with parental support and have been diagnosed as having a true gender conflict, doctors can prescribe a nonmedical transition to the true gender the child feels that they are. This allows the child to socialize with other children of their correct gender and experience all the social effects other children experience when growing up in their true gender. When the child approaches puberty, they can be prescribed hormone blockers for the hormones appropriate to their birth sex, and they can be administered hormones appropriate for their gender identity. For example, a young male child experiencing feelings that they are female can be given testosterone blockers (to prevent the emergence of male characteristics) and estrogen (to encourage the development of female characteristics). The effects of these medicines are reversible, and if the child decides when they become an adult that all of this was wrong, they can resume living in their assigned birth gender. However, suppose they desire to keep the gender that they have been expressing as a child and teenager. In that case, they then have the option of undergoing gender confirmation surgery to match their body's characteristics with their true gender.

These steps can allow the person to grow and experience their true gender as they mature. It will allow them to be married, if they so desire, and to assume their proper natural role in the family. This avoids the situation I had, involving a wife and child in my conflicts. I hope that as time goes on and medical science progresses, and society accepts the resolution of gender identity conflicts, more children will assume their proper role in society and fewer people will have to go through the turmoil Jan and I went through.

Parents must support their children as they begin to explore their gender identity. Although most babies' sex can be determined at birth, their gender is what they perceive as they grow. It has always troubled me that so many parents are "celebrating" what they describe as "gender reveal parties" before the birth of their children. What they are revealing, at best, is the child's expected sex and assigned gender, not their gender identity. As www.healthychildren.org, a website of the American Academy of Pediatrics, notes:

Gender identity typically develops in stages:

- *Around age two: Children become conscious of the physical differences between boys and girls.*

- *Before their third birthday: Most children can easily label themselves as either a boy or a girl.*

- *By age four: Most children have a stable sense of their gender identity.*

During this same time of life, children learn gender role behavior; that is, doing "things that boys do" or "things that girls do." However, cross-gender preferences and play are a normal part of gender development and exploration, regardless of their future gender identity.[19]

Because of this development process, parents must allow their children to experiment. If there appears to be an issue of cross-gender concern, they should contact a qualified gender specialist or clinic to evaluate the steps that need to be taken.

It must be noted here that religious leaders, priests, pastors, etc., are usually not qualified to evaluate cross-gender behavior. What religious groups call "conversion therapy" has been proven to be more harmful and has no known ability to change a person's gender identity or sexual orientation. Attempts to force children to live according to their assigned birth genders, rather than their own perceptions of their gender identities, are far more harmful. I am living proof that no amount of prayer and effort can change your gender identity. It just results in a lifetime of turmoil and broken relationships. The attempts of legislatures across the country to force children to live as their assigned gender by withdrawing medical support and creating penalties for doctors who treat gender conflicted children are doomed to failure and will only increase the number of suicides and broken lives.

In the last decade, some politicians, at national, state, and local levels, encouraged by various right-wing Evangelical organizations, have had the transgender community in their crosshairs. Many attempts have been made to legislate the ability of transgender persons to participate in sports at all levels and ages. These efforts have denied the real effects of hormones on the human body. Young, prepubescent children do not have any significant strength or ability levels beyond

---

[19] Gender Identity Development in Children - HealthyChildren.org

normal variations. There are large-sized, strong young girls, just as there are similar size and strength characteristics among boys. We would not permit a limitation on the ability of a bigger, stronger girl to participate in girls' sports in her age group, nor would we eliminate a smaller boy from participating in age-appropriate boys' sports. We might make appropriate accommodations for size and strength differences, but we would not eliminate any possibility of their playing sports.

Not until the onset of puberty, with the effect of hormones, do significant differences in size and strength occur. The effect of testosterone on teenage boys not only deepens the voice, but also causes an increase in size and muscle mass. The effect of estrogen on girls causes the physical changes associated with puberty, including maturation of the breasts, ovaries, uterus, and vagina, as well as bringing on a girl's first menstrual period. It also increases fat deposits and reduces muscle mass.

There is no question that the effects of hormones on cisgender teenagers going through puberty mandate a separation between girls' and boys' sports activities that involve physical activity. However, separation would not be warranted for trans children who have been prescribed hormone blockers and hormones appropriate for their gender identity. A child designated as male at birth, transitioning to female, would be taking testosterone blockers (to eliminate the effects of testosterone on their voice, size, and muscle mass) along with estrogen (to encourage fat deposit buildup and limit size and muscle mass). The results are a person who has the desired size and strength body characteristics of a female of their age level. Such a person should not be forced to participate in sports with boys of their age because it would be too dangerous. Similarly, a child designated as female at birth, transitioning to male, would be taking estrogen blockers (to limit the effects of estrogen on their bodies) and testosterone (to encourage a deeper vocal level and an increase in size and muscle mass). The results are a person who has the desired body characteristics of a male of their age level. Such a person should not be forced to participate in sports with girls of their age because it would be too dangerous.

Science is well aware of all of these facts. That is why major medical and pediatric societies have opposed the various legislative efforts to regulate the treatment that doctors can give and the sports activities allowed for transgender children. It is clear that efforts to legislate transgender treatment are motivated by transphobia and have no place in the ethical treatment of the transgender condition.

Jan and Barry Manilow

Any attempt to discuss the life that Jan and I had together would be lacking if I left out Jan's love of Barry Manilow's music and its influence on her. I also appreciated Barry's music and went to many concerts with her, but clearly she was more passionate about her devotion to his music. Jan always said that she loved Barry's music and had followed his career since his first big hit, "Mandy," in 1974. Jan was motivated to re-engage with Barry in 2005 when she met a member of one of the Barry Manilow International Fan Club (BMIFC) local chapters in a support group for trans spouses that our counselor conducted. After one of their support-group meetings, they talked about Barry, and Jan joined the local chapter and became interested in attending one of his concerts.

Jan began to reconnect with her love of Manilow's music. As she reconnected, she found that his music gave her comfort as she struggled through my transition. In 2005 Barry had begun appearing regularly at the Las Vegas Hilton. Our son became aware of Jan's interest and found out that Barry was in residence in Las Vegas at the Hilton where he performed. As an anniversary gift, he gave Jan two, third-row tickets to Barry's concert on Friday, November 4, 2005, as well as plane tickets to Las Vegas and a hotel stay at the Mirage hotel.

We both enjoyed that first concert so much that we went to the box office after the concert and bought balcony tickets for both of his Saturday concerts the next night. We also switched hotels to the Hilton for Saturday and changed our return flights to Sunday afternoon. Jan thoroughly enjoyed both Saturday shows. At the second show, during the "Copa" number, when Barry and the singers performed from a platform above the crowd, Jan went down the aisle to the front of the balcony and blew Barry a kiss, which he acknowledged by returning an "air kiss" to her.

Jan waiting for her first Barry concert. / Barry at Jan's first concert. / Jan with Barry's picture outside the theatre.

I also enjoyed his concerts, but, clearly, Barry's positive outlook expressed in so many of his songs helped Jan significantly as she processed my gender transition. One of her favorite songs was "I Made It Through the Rain." It expressed a positive outlook on surviving the trials of life and gave Jan encouragement that she could make it. In 2006 Jan wrote the following birthday message to Barry on one of the fan message boards:

Words can't adequately express the impact that you and your music have had on my life. Perhaps the closest I can come is "no one will EVER touch me more." You truly are a gift from God to the world, and, indeed, have your own place deep in my soul. Your music and passion have saved my sanity, if not my life, several times since "Mandy." Because of you, I have made many wonderful friends who have become like family, especially in the past eighteen months.

We continued to attend as many of his concerts as we could. I was with Jan for most of the shows. According to the records she kept, I missed ten of the concerts she attended. She went with other friends and also to fan-club conventions without me. Jan kept a running log of the concerts she attended, and her last, her fifty-seventh, was on February 11, 2016, at Northern Kentucky University BB&T Center in Highland Heights, Kentucky. We had one more scheduled in Nashville the next day, but I was recovering from gall bladder surgery, and we couldn't make the trip down there, so we gave our tickets to friends who lived in Nashville.

The Northern Kentucky concert was also important because, as we were leaving, we were stopped by another concertgoer, Farryn, who was curious about us two old fogies toddling along with our walkers. We told her a bit of our story, and she asked if we would like to participate in a conference she was working on for NGLCC (then National Gay and Lesbian Chamber of Commerce, now National LGBT Chamber of Commerce). Her company flew us out in August 2016 to the conference in Palm Springs, California, where Jan and I told our story in a conference session. We were later to participate in a documentary NGLCC produced entitled *Families Like Yours*.

We both met Barry twice in what was called "Platinum Meet and Greet" sessions. We donated to the Manilow Music Project for the opportunity to meet with him. We could have gone in together to meet him, but Jan insisted on meeting him by herself. She told me that she didn't want to share any of her time with Barry.

Jan and Barry at first Platinum April 20, 2007. / Jan and Barry
at second Platinum March 20, 2009.

At Jan's second Platinum, she got him to dance with her,
which she had hoped for at each concert if our seats were
close to the front.

I suspect some of Jan's concern about sharing her time
with Barry may have come from an incident we had when
we had front-row, side-stage seats during one of our early
concerts in April 2006. Barry had a portion of the concert in
which he went to our side of the stage to what he called his
"piano bar" set. When he arrived there, he would take off his
jacket, hang it up, and put on a white jacket for that segment.
He would always ask one of the front-row ladies to help him
on with his jacket. This lady was known among the fans as
his "jacket girl."

When we bought the tickets for those seats, Jan began
obsessing about what she would say when she was picked
to be the jacket girl. Unfortunately, when it came to that
moment in the concert, Barry looked at the two of us in the
front row and picked me to help him put on his jacket. I was
stunned. I had not even thought about the possibility that
he would pick me and had given no consideration as to what
I would say. I fumbled through the process of helping him
on with his jacket and mumbled some answers to his ques-

tions as best as I could. He went on with the concert, but Jan was very upset with me. Jan later told me I should have told him to pick her. My response was that I could not think of saying no to anything Barry requested of me. It was clear that she was not happy with me, however. Also, my name was mud among several of the local BMIFC members who were in attendance.

Jan was well known among the BMIFC members and Barry's staff, band, and background singers. After our first trip to Las Vegas to see Barry, Jan returned to work to find her cubicle decorated with various Manilow paraphernalia. One of the things she received was a pair of maracas that she began to carry with her to most concerts. Jan shook them vigorously during some of the songs, but especially during the Copacabana performance. She became known as "Barry's maraca woman." Most of his band, along with Barry and his background singers, knew when she was there.

Jan and her maracas during Copa

One of Jan's favorite people among Barry's onstage performers was his choreographer and background singer, Kye Brackett. We met Kye several times and had lunch and post-show snacks with him on several occasions. He also came out to meet us following several concerts. One of the most important times was following a show in August 2010. Jan was scheduled for her mastectomy surgery for her breast cancer closely following that concert, and she was very nervous. Kye met with her for thirty minutes and encouraged her. It was a very meaningful experience for Jan, and he helped her to get through her surgery.

Jan and Kye, August 2010. / Barry and Kye during August 2010 concert.

Jan was well known among many of the BMIFC members. She had been active in several of the fan club online chat groups. When I began to gather some of the information I needed to write this book, I ran across several files from Jan's chat groups; they were logs of conversations she had with friends. I had avoided those groups because I wanted them to be a place where Jan could speak freely to her friends, without concern that I was listening. Also, I wanted her Barry Manilow experience to be as much as possible apart from our gender issues. If I had been involved in the online groups, my transition could have become a matter of discussion and sidetracked the discussions about Barry and his music.

Postscript

Jan is gone. I have tried in my writing to be as faithful to her feelings as I could be. However, even in the best of marriages, some things are kept back between partners. So, I pray that she would approve of these efforts. She and I were "Velcroed at the hip" for almost fifty-five years, so I feel as if I have lost the better part of me.

This effort to put our story down in writing was something that many people suggested to us through the years. Jan and I discussed a book several times, but she didn't want to write it, and I didn't want to do it without her voice being heard. Cancer decided for us when it took her from me on July 23, 2019, so I've done my best. I hope this is useful to someone.

Jan's legacy to our grandchildren was her life and her efforts to uncover our ancestors through Ancestry. Jan's stepsister has taken over her efforts for her mother's family, and our son has taken over those efforts for her father's family. I guess my efforts for posterity can be this book.

Diane DeLap, October 1, 2021

Addendum

Letter to Jan's Mother

Saturday, March 26, 2005

To Jan's Mother,

First, I want to thank you for some advice you gave Jan before we were married. You told her, "When you have problems, don't come running back to me because you're on your own. You made your bed; now lie in it. I give you six months." Those words told both of us that we were on our own and that, when we encountered problems in our marriage, we would have to solve them together. We could not look to our parents to help us solve them. Over the past forty plus years, there have been numerous times when those words have brought us back together to work our way through the many and different problems we encountered as a couple.

Certainly, those words were fresh in our minds when Jan discovered my cross-gender behavior six months after we were married. At the time, neither of us understood what was driving my feelings, but we clearly understood that, whatever was happening, we were on our own to deal with the situation. We stayed together, and through the years, there were many days and nights that we argued, fought, cried, prayed, studied, and stayed up all night and exhausted ourselves working through our feelings together.

Through the years, we discovered that, whatever was going on, no amount of self-control on my part, love on Jan's part, prayers on both our parts, or dedication to God's work would make the feelings go away. As I began to study the Bible more, I discovered Paul's words regarding his "thorn in the flesh":

> *Three times I pleaded with the Lord to take it away from me. But he said to me, "My grace is sufficient for you, for my power is made perfect in weakness." Therefore, I will boast all the more gladly about my weaknesses, so that Christ's power may rest on me. That is why, for Christ's sake, I delight in weaknesses, in insults, in hardships, in persecutions, in difficulties. For when I am weak, then I am strong.*[20]

I drew strength and understanding from Paul's struggles with his "thorn." And I learned that not all prayers are answered with a yes. Sometimes God says no and wants us to draw our strength from Him, instead of relying on our own to solve what we perceive as problems.

I learned that sometimes what we feel are our problems are instead opportunities to serve God in a new and different way. I began to understand what many of Christ's disciples had to find out in the early days of the church, that our understanding of what is right and wrong is not always God's.

Like Philip, who had to be directed by an angel to a eunuch, the transgender person of his time, who in response to the

---

[20] Bible quotations are from the New International Version.

question "Look, here is water. Why shouldn't I be baptized?" mirrored God's acceptance of that outcast of society and the religious of his time by leading him into the waters of baptism.

Like Saul, who had to be struck blind before he could learn that those he was persecuting, at the direction of the Jewish leadership, were the ones who were following the way of God.

Like Peter, who had to be told three times, "Do not call anything impure that God has made clean." He had to learn that he needed to accept as a child of God someone he had been taught by the religious leaders of his time was sinful, and to accept Cornelius, a gentile, as a fellow follower of Christ.

We do not always know the mind of God, and sometimes He has to push us into the place He wants us in order to learn the lesson He wants us to, so that we can be the people He wants us to be.

Jan tells me that you are extremely angry for what you think I've "done to this family." First, let me say that you must know that God does not want you to be angry. Paul tells us, "Get rid of all bitterness, rage and anger, brawling, and slander, along with every form of malice," and "You must rid yourselves of all such things as these: anger, rage, malice, slander, and filthy language from your lips." James also suggests, "Everyone should be quick to listen, slow to speak, and slow to become angry, for man's anger does not bring about the righteous life that God desires." Your anger sorrows me, and I will pray that you may be able to overcome it.

To help you with that, let me assure you that I have not done this. What I have done is acknowledge a lifelong condition and deal with it honestly and openly. Jan and I together reached the decision that now was the time for me to begin dealing with this. I have struggled with this all my life, but rather than abandon my wife and child, as many with my condition do, I remained and supported Jan and our son through his childhood, teenage, and young-adult years until he was on his own, had broken ties with us, and had begun to establish his own family.

We realized that our decision would certainly affect many within our family. Still, we hoped and prayed that those who had declared through the years that they loved us and cared for us would, as they learned about it, take the time to try to get past the message of the "world" that some types of people are to be hated, and as Paul suggests, "Each of you should look not only to your interests, but also to the interests of others. Your attitude should be the same as that of Christ Jesus." Paul was talking about Christ's willingness to give up the glory He had in heaven to die for us on the cross. Still, certainly, if our "attitude is the same as Christ," that would extend to His example of consistent love and acceptance of the outcast and downtrodden of His time. We had hoped that you, who have declared your dedication to God as well as your love for us, would be able to overcome the judgmental, Pharisaical approach, which so much of the Fundamentalist Church has taken on, and would open yourself up to trying to understand what the issue is all about.

I no more decided to be the way I am than does a blind, deaf, or disabled child. Perhaps it's more similar to things like ADD or other conditions related to the brain and genetics than an external, visible defect like blindness. Even in Jesus's time, the perception of the Church was that deformities are the result of sin:

As he went along, he saw a man blind from birth. His disciples asked him, "Rabbi, who sinned, this man or his parents, that he was born blind"

"Neither this man nor his parents sinned," said Jesus, "but this happened so that the work of God might be displayed in his life."

In times past, the church and the Bible were used to support the bigotries of racism and sexism. But just as society and the church have been reluctant to accept differences like ADD, bipolarism, and depression as treatable lifelong conditions, someday they will accept the growing body of science that understands that our perception of gender is distinct from the physical characteristics of our body. Despite the perception in Western society that gender and sex are fixed and immutable, science is coming to understand that God's creation is far more varied in humans, just as it is with plants and animals. Despite our attempt to simplify human creation into the two categories of Genesis, evidence is growing that there are infinite, though small in number, variations in both gender perception and physical sex characteristics. The existence of intersex (hermaphrodite) conditions in newborn babies is in the range of one in 3,000. The incidence of transgender characteristics, because it is not physically perceived, is not known because so many of us live in fear of the church and society's condemnation of us; we don't reveal ourselves. More and more of us are starting to come out in the open, however.

How could you think that I would willingly decide to put myself and my family in this situation? I knew the consequences far better than most transgender people do. I knew that most transgender people lose friends, family, spouses, children, jobs, everything, and even their lives when they transition. I hoped that my friends and family would love and care for me enough to learn of the torment I went through and accept me as I know Christ has. I knew it would be difficult, but Jan convinced me that the alternative, suicide, would have hurt my friends and family more. Imagine my surprise and hurt when I heard that your preference would have been that I "disappeared."

The only way anyone truly "disappears" from this world is through death, and, certainly, that would have been the way I would have chosen to disappear. Rather than try to overcome your fear and bigotry, you would prefer that I kill myself to take myself out of your life. I believed you all through the years when you said you cared about me and appreciated the care I took of your daughter. But when it came time for her to take care of me, and when you saw my imperfections, you would rather have me "disappear."

I'm also sorry to hear that you believe that I'm selfish in dealing with this condition. Maybe you think it was selfish of me to endure the torment that was my daily life to support your daughter and raise your grandchild. I find it hard to understand how asking for the right to live a third of my life in peace is selfish, when I willingly gave up that peace for the other two-thirds of my life for the benefit of others. Perhaps the fact that the two people most impacted, Jan and our son, are willing to try to sacrifice for me in return doesn't matter to you. It's not easy for them, but rather than try to give them your support, understanding, and encouragement, you criticize and berate them because of what you perceive is my selfishness in doing this to your family. Who's being selfish? Me by my transition? Or you by your reaction to it? Maybe it's not my transition that's hurting your family, but you by your reaction to it.

I'm also sorry you feel that I would go to hell if I died today because I'm sinning. I'm sorry, not because I believe that, but because I'm sorry that a lifetime of hearing of the Grace of God in Christ has left you unaware of it. Of course, I'm sinning. So are you. So are your other children. So is Jan. So are we all. The Bible says, "all have sinned and fall short of the glory of God, and are justified freely by His grace through the redemption that came by Christ Jesus." All means all, even you and me.

I have concluded that there is nothing in the Bible that declares with any certainty that my transgender condition is a sin. There are some, a very few, scriptures that in some English translations reflect Western society's negativity toward the transgender condition. However, when you study those verses, particularly in the original languages, you discover that the translators may be presenting their prejudices rather than revealing the text's true meaning. Unfortunately, the Bible is not as clear on this topic as you appear to believe it is.

In addition, I don't pretend to know the mind of God in His judgment of us, and I would suggest that you take that approach as well. Jesus consistently spoke against the human tendency to judge others:

Do not judge, or you too will be judged. For in the same way you judge others, you will be judged, and with the measure you use, it will be measured to you. Why do you look at the speck of sawdust in your brother's eye and pay no attention to the plank in your own eye?

He also declares that it is God's responsibility, not ours, to judge the unrighteous:

And if any man hears my words, and believe not, I judge him not: for I came not to judge the world, but to save the world. He that rejecteth me, and receiveth not my words, hath one that judgeth him: the word that I have spoken, the same shall judge him in the last day.

I would be careful in applying Fundamentalist judgmental approaches to others since it's clear that "in the same way you judge others, you will be judged." If in your actions you use the law and not grace as a measure of others, perhaps that same measure will be used in your judgment. I will pray that your eyes will be opened to the dangers of such an approach before that final day, and that you accept that the Grace of Christ is available to all, regardless of how sinful you perceive their lives to be.

Finally, I need to say a few words about my decision to write you this letter. When Jan came home from work last week in tears, when she cried through the night and sat on the side of the bed in the morning in tears, my first inclination was to pick up the phone and call you and express my feelings to you. Jan asked me not to, and as I have throughout this process, I respected her decision. I also came to understand that it might be better to express my feelings in writing. I might be less likely to say something, through the frustration, that I would regret later. In addition, you would have an opportunity to read, and reread if you want to, what I have to say. With her agreement, I have written this letter to you.

She chose to tell you of our situation, believing that she would find love and understanding. She now believes that decision was a mistake. She is going through torment not only from your words and from bearing the brunt of your hatred of me, but also in self-recrimination for revealing our situation to you. I do not share her opinion that this was a mistake. She decided after many hours of prayer and discussion with God as well as me. I don't believe that decisions made like that can be wrong. God is giving us all a chance to grow from this. We do not yet know the result of this decision. I will continue to pray for both you and Jan that you will be at peace with God and each other.

CPSIA information can be obtained
at www.ICGtesting.com
Printed in the USA
BVHW092134040222
627691BV00004B/6